Pagan Portals
The Cailleach

Pagan Portals
The Cailleach

Rachel Patterson

MOON
BOOKS

Winchester, UK
Washington, USA

First published by Moon Books, 2016
Moon Books is an imprint of John Hunt Publishing Ltd., Laurel House, Station Approach,
Alresford, Hants, SO24 9JH, UK
office1@jhpbooks.net
www.johnhuntpublishing.com
www.moon-books.net

For distributor details and how to order please visit the 'Ordering' section on our website.

Text copyright: Rachel Patterson 2015

ISBN: 978 1 78535 322 2
Library of Congress Control Number: 2016934235

A CIP catalogue record for this book is available from the British Library.

Design: Stuart Davies

Printed and bound by CPI Group (UK) Ltd, Croydon, CR0 4YY, UK

We operate a distinctive and ethical publishing philosophy in all
areas of our business, from our global network of authors to
production and worldwide distribution.

CONTENTS

Who am I?

I am a witch...have been for a very long time, not the green skinned warty kind obviously...the real sort, but I am also a working wife and mother who has also been lucky enough to write and have published a book or three. I love to learn, I love to study and have done so from books, online resources, schools and wonderful mentors over the years and still continue to learn each and every day, but have learnt the most from actually getting outside and doing it.

I like to laugh...and eat cake...

I am High Priestess of the Kitchen Witch Coven and an Elder at the online Kitchen Witch School of Natural Witchcraft.

My craft is a combination of old religion witchcraft, kitchen witchery, hedge witchery and folk magic. My heart is that of a Kitchen Witch. I am blessed with a wonderful husband, lovely children, a fabulous family and good friends.

Bibliography

Pagan Portals – Kitchen Witchcraft
Grimoire of a Kitchen Witch
Pagan Portals – Hoodoo Folk Magic
Pagan Portals – Moon Magic
A Kitchen Witch's World of Magical Plants & Herbs
A Kitchen Witch's World of Magical Foods
Pagan Portals – Meditation
The Art of Ritual
Arc of the Goddess (co-written with Tracey Roberts)

Websites

My website: www.rachelpatterson.co.uk
Facebook: www.facebook.com/rachelpattersonbooks
My personal blog: www.tansyfiredragon.blogspot.co.uk

Email: tansyfiredragon@yahoo.com
www.kitchenwitchhearth.net
www.kitchenwitchuk.blogspot.co.uk
www.facebook.com/kitchenwitchuk
www.thekitchenwitchcauldron.blogspot.co.uk

With huge thanks to my lovely daughter Emma (age 15) who sketched the image of the Cailleach for the front cover and to my husband for working his computer graphics magic to make it into a book cover.

Author's Comment

The Cailleach came to me many years ago when I had been on the witchcraft pathway for six or seven years and had worked with a lot of different deities. Although most of them came from the Celtic pantheon I have always been open to whatever deity makes itself known; each encounter has been for a very good reason. I wasn't looking for a matron goddess, in fact I was reading a work of fiction, a pretty good 'twists and turns' mystical thriller where the heroine of the story was assisted by a blue-faced hag who hung in the shadows; she was named the Cailleach Bheur. After reading that book I kept hearing and seeing her name mentioned (obviously not in the supermarket, but in other things I read and as I surfed the net). This goddess was most definitely trying to get my attention so I started on a journey with her that I have never regretted, not even on the bad days when she kicks my butt because I don't listen...

In writing this book I have drawn upon myths, legends and folklore because although there are one or two historic documents that mention her name, most of her 'history' has been passed down through storytelling and folk tales. Most of the written information is relatively recent, as in the past couple of centuries. The rest is just given to us in the form of folk stories and hints in the ancient monuments and the names of places that seem to be associated with her.

I can only present you with the information I have discovered, it is up to you to choose which pieces resonate with you and which don't. I have also added a chapter on how to work with her on a magical basis – this is taken from my own personal experience with her.

She has many myths and legends all passed down verbally and most of them have the same theme, that of renewal, each generation adding or changing bits of the story to suit the times.

I think this has happened particularly with the Cailleach, turning her from a goddess of creation, wisdom, harmony and rebirth into a dark and evil hag. She does seem to have been given the 'Hollywood' treatment making her out to be the 'bad guy' and trapping her in the confines of winter. But she is so much more...

Whether you would like to work with the Cailleach on a magical basis or are just interested in her legends, I hope you will enjoy this introduction and then seek her out. Please bear in mind that each and every one of us has our own personal pathway and we will all have individual and unique experiences with deity. Nothing is right or wrong there is only YOUR experience.

And to help...her name can be pronounced in a different ways, depending on what part of the world you are from and what accent you use:

kye-luhkh
cally-ach-y
cay-loch
coy-luck
ky-och
cail-leach
kay-lex

Birth of the Cailleach

She is ancient...
She is the landscape beneath our feet
She is the mountains and the hills
She is the rock and stone that leads down to the shore
She is wisdom
She is knowledge
She is mysteries
She is the old hag
She is The Cailleach

Within the pages of this book I hope to give you an introduction to the mysteries, myths, legends and magic of the ancient hag goddess the Cailleach.

The Cailleach – goddess of the ancestors, wisdom that comes with age, the weather, time, shape-shifting and winter.

She is said to have shaped the landscape by dropping boulders from her apron, which given that she is often portrayed as a giant should have been a fairly easy task. Later on stories also began to surface that reported the Devil as being the one with an apron who drops stones to shape the landscape. Not sure the image of the Devil wearing a pinny with the apron strings flapping in the breeze works for me, but it may have been an attempt by early Christianity to cover up the pagan stories of the Cailleach.

Her time is Samhain to Beltane, which is when she is at her most powerful – and powerful she most certainly is for in my experience she is a strong, feisty, no-nonsense, and kick-bottom goddess with a wicked sense of humour. Towards the end of autumn when the weather starts to get that clear, fresh and chilly air you can feel her draw near.

Often referred to as a Neolithic goddess, her origins seem to lie in ancient Britain. However, traces of her can be found across Europe, still as part of Celtic tribal history, but also in places such as Greece, Spain and Portugal. Some suggest that she was originally a Spanish princess named Beara and others that she originated from the Hindu mother goddess Kali, but some believe she travelled across from the continent, who is right? (I don't have the actual answer to that question...)

Although she rarely appears in myths with other deities she is occasionally linked with the goddess Brighid/Bride as her opposite. In a couple of legends she is also said to have married the Celtic sea god Manannan. She is usually put into the Celtic pantheon (I have done so myself on occasion) possibly just to put her somewhere, but there are traces of her long before the Celts. She is, as far as I can make out, one of the most ancient deities and has survived for thousands of years. An old Irish poem states: 'There are three great ages; the age of the yew tree, the age of the eagle, the age of the Cailleach.'

The word Cailleach has several meanings or translations such as:

Hag
Crone
Old woman
Veiled one
Witch
Older wiser woman
Biting old woman
Old wife

In Gaelic there seems to be suggestion of a link between the word 'Cailleach' and the word for 'chalice'. The chalice possibly being later thought of as a cauldron, which is a symbol for rebirth and symbolic of the womb.

In most texts the word 'Cailleach' seems to translate as 'veiled one' and the prefix 'Caill' also means a 'covering'. It suggests that an older woman wore a 'cover chief' or 'calle' upon their head, perhaps referring to a veil or headscarf, and of course the veil also symbolises hidden mysteries.

There are many, many stories about a Cailleach, whether they are one and the same figure or a group of figures I will let you decide. She may just have had slightly different names in each region such as:

Cailleach Bheur – the sharp Cailleach/genteel old lady (Scotland)
Cailleach ny Groamagh – the old gloomy woman (Manx)
Cailleach Groarnagh – old woman of spells (Manx)
Cailleach Beara/Bheare/Bearra (Ireland)
Caillagh ny Gueshag – old woman of the spells
Cailleach Uragaig (Isle of Colonsay, Scotland)
Cailleach Bheirre/Beira – the sharp Cailleach (Ireland)
Cailleach Beinne Bric/na Bric – old woman of the speckled
  mountain/protector of the deer (Scotland)
Cailleach Mor/Mhore – great old woman (Scotland)
Cailleach Mhor Nam Fiadh – the Great Cailleach of the deer
  (Scotland)
Cailleach na Mointeach – Cailleach of the Moors (Scotland)
Cailleach Usig – water Cailleach
Carlin (Scotland)
Beira (Scotland)
Cally Berry (Northern Ireland)
The Hag of Beare/Digne (Ireland)
Cailleach Nollaigh – Christmas old wife (Scotland)
Mag Moullach
Gentle Annie (NE Scotland)
Bronach or Brenach – ugliness (W Ireland)
The Blue Hag
The Bear Goddess
The Boar Goddess

Owl-faced
Ancient Woman
The Woman of Stones

She is probably most well known for her landscaping, with many mountains, caves, rivers and landmarks named after her. She is therefore strongly associated with the elements of both earth and water. As a water goddess the Cailleach rules over lakes, rivers, oceans, streams and wells, and holds responsibility for floods as she also controls the weather, particularly storms. Stories of the Cailleach storming (pun intended) down the mountainside in a fury hurling lightning rods and bolts of thunder are plenty.

She is also linked with the wise woman who played the role of midwife and layer-out of the dead. Several stories I found linked her to Christian times when it was said she appeared as a nun...although this could be confusion caused by her Gaelic name meaning 'hood' or 'veiled one', which after Christianity arrived was the term given to nuns reflecting the hooded wimples they wore.

The Cailleach is at her most powerful during the winter months, bringing the cold weather, icy winds and snow with her. She is said to often ride a wolf (sometimes a wild pig) across the sky bringing the snow and riding the wolf through the lands crushing any signs of plant life. But she is also seen as the midwife for the dying year, keeping the seeds of new life safe and warm beneath the earth, caring for them throughout the winter months so that they may become new life in the spring.

The 25th of March was known as Latha na Caillich, Cailleach Day or Lady Day. Right up to the 17th century in Scotland this date was celebrated as New Year's Day and contests would be held to drive out the winter hag.

On 1st May on the Isle of Man, mock fights were held between the harsh forces of winter and the promising light of summer, with summer always winning of course. This represented the hag goddess fighting with her sisters over the rights of the land.

In February (around Imbolc) in Orkney, the Gyros festival happens where two of the boys in the village dress up as hags and chase the younger children around town trying to catch them and hit them with ropes. The name Gyros may be connected to the Gyre of Carling, one of the Cailleach's many guises.

On 1st November the Reign of the Old Woman Cailleach was celebrated in Celtic countries (in Ireland it was known as 'day of the banshees'). Another celebration is held on the eve of Imbolc to mark 'the end of the Cailleach'.

In Spain the feast of St Agatha was celebrated on 5th February to represent the changing of the seasons. The saint was depicted as an old hag who carries winter away in her bag, possibly a link to the Cailleach.

All of these celebrations and festivals seem to be in line with the arrival of spring and the banishing of winter (and then vice versa), which echoes the theme of the Cailleach as a goddess of winter.

As a crone goddess she is often depicted as the stereotypical hag figure often with a blue hue to her skin perhaps symbolising the wisdom of old age, winter, death and experience, but it may also link to the blue woad that the Picts painted themselves with. Her dark skin may be the blackness of the caves, the dark storm or the midnight sky. She is sometimes seen with just one eye that could perhaps represent the weak winter sun, but also her seer abilities and her supernatural influence. It may even be a representation of the moon. Irish myths often carry stories of heroes who only have one eye (along with other abnormalities and disfigurements). The Formorians (Balor springs to mind), who are often seen as the enemy, often have these characteristics. The Cailleach was said to have had many giant sons known as Fooar, perhaps linked to the name Formorians? Folklore tells that a seeker can find divine inspiration by standing on one foot and closing one eye (sounds like a way of falling over to me), but this perhaps reflects the deformities of the gods.

The Yellow Book of Lecan (c. 1400AD) states that the Cailleach had seven youthful periods, married seven husbands (each who grew old and died) and had 50 foster children who founded many tribes and nations. It also tells that the Cailleach Bheara was also known as Bui or Boi meaning 'yellow'.

She is sometimes said to have red teeth and nearly always has white hair. This woman has lived through it all, seen it all, done it all and got the T-shirt.

In a few stories the Cailleach also displays her abilities as a seer and often as a trickster – most definitely with a wickedly naughty side.

She is also said to be a goddess who governs dreams and inner realities and she is the goddess of the sacred hill, the Sidhe – the place where we enter into the realm of Faerie. She has also been connected to the 'bean sidhe' (or banshee) in some tales.

There is mention on occasion in stories that the Cailleach was once part of a trinity with her two sisters and known as a triple goddess, the Cailleach Bheare being joined by Cailleach Bolus and Cailleach Corca Duibhne. In Scotland they spoke of Beur Cailleachan in the plural as powerful beings that lived in the lochs. A Gaelic song mentions the three Cailleachan of the Scottish Hebrides.

Some of the stories tell that Cailleach Bheare is the wife of the god Lugh, but that she outlives many husbands and remains youthful while they grow old and pass away.

In her right hand, some stories say that she carries a magic rod (or hammer), which she uses to turn the blades of grass into ice. Sometimes it is described as a staff that she bangs on the ground to bring the cold and winter. It is said once signs of spring start she flies into a rage throwing her wand beneath a holly tree...giving the reason why grass doesn't usually grow under holly trees.

If you listen to all the stories the Cailleach has lived in many places, which include a lot of mountains such as Ben Nevis, Ben Wyvis, Ben Breac, Ben Cruachan, the Paps of Jura, Schiehallion, Lochnagar, Caistel Caillich and Beinn na Caillich – all hill tops.

She can appear to be fearsome and she is most definitely powerful as the hag of winter, woman of stones, bone mother, a goddess of death, the dark mother, the harvest goddess, an ancestress who rules the dark half of the year and is as ancient as the earth itself, but she does have a nurturing side; she is the spirit of the land and allows us to peek at the wisdom we need to let go of what no longer serves us and look forward to what is yet to come. Let's not forget that to have rebirth there must be death first. Without the Cailleach culling the plants in the winter they would not survive the harsh weather.

The Cailleach in Scotland

In folk stories from Scotland it is said that the Cailleach rises at Samhain and brings with her the snow, ice and harsh weather until Imbolc when she turns back into stone. The stone remains damp as it contains her life essence. She is also said to spend her entire time chasing after her son or in some stories her lover.

She is also considered to be the daughter of Grainne, or the winter sun. The old Celtic calendar had two suns, 'the big sun', which shone from Beltane to Samhain, and 'the little sun', which shone from Samhain to Beltane eve.

There are many stories and place names associated with the Cailleach in Scotland and the Hebridean islands. In some parts of Scotland she is known as the Carlin and occasionally referred to as Queen of the Witches.

She is said to have created a huge amount of the Scottish landscape by wading through the surrounding waters up and down the country dropping large boulders from her creel (apron) to make the islands and using smaller rocks to create the mountains. Some of these are Beinn Cailleach Bheur in Argyllshire, Beinn na Caillich on the Isle of Skye, Loch Awe in Argyll and Bute and mountains in Lochaber. A large furrow down the side of Beinn na Cailliach called Sgriob na Calliach (furrow of the Cailleach) is said to have been created when she stumbled and slid down the hill. Other place names in Scotland refer to her, such as Cailleach Vear – a rock off Mull, Sgeir Cailleach – Jura, Ceum na Caillich – Arran, Cailleach Head – Ross, Carlin's Loup near Carlop and Creagan Biorach na Cailliche Moire on Lewis to name but a few.

One story tells of the Cailleach Bheur as a blue-faced hag of winter who ages in reverse. She starts out old, gnarled and ugly and gradually becomes young and beautiful, perhaps symbolising the progression of winter to spring.

She is known sometimes as 'Grandmother of the Clans' or 'Ancestress of the Caledonii Tribe'. The legends of the Caledonii tribe talk about the 'bringer of the ice mountains', the great blue old woman of the highlands. She was a mountain giantess who protected the tribe and kept them safe.

Scotland was called Caledonia, a Latin name given by the Romans; some suggest that this translates as 'the land given by Cailleach'. I suspect the name referred to the Pictish tribe – the Caledonii that lived in the area during the Iron Age and Roman times. The Roman historian Tacticus tells that the Caledonii had 'red hair and large limbs' and were a fierce people who were quick to fight off invaders.

The tribes inhabiting Caledonia flew to arms, and with great prepa-rations, made greater by the rumours which always exaggerate the unknown, themselves advanced to attack our fortresses...
Tacitus, *Life of Cnaeus Julius Agricola*, c AD98

The Cailleach Life Story

She was the first living being in Scotland after the ice had melted, thousands of years ago. The Cailleach had the first plaid and being the first it had no checks, stripes or colour and was as pure white as the snow. She would spread the plaid on the hills to create the snow-covered tops. Being immortal she was unable to die, but grew weary with living and changed herself into a giant, laying herself down for an endless sleep.

Time passed – months, years, decades – and soil collected over her body and the plants started to grow creating a glen, which became a great mountain.

And when the mists draw across the mountain it is said that the Cailleach has drawn a veil across her face.

Mountain Springs

Mountain springs were said to be a sanctuary for the Cailleach, she would visit them to renew her strength or to perform rites of passage for the seasons. One story said that the Cailleach came in the dead of the night to the Well of Youth (near Loch Ba of Mull) and drank 'before bird tasted water or dog was heard to bark'. Her longevity was believed to have come from the water of life. However, one of the stories tells that a dog barked before the Cailleach had bent to the water and she crumbled into dust.

The Shepherd and the Dog

Here is a slightly different version of the Mountain Springs story.

A shepherd, knowing that winter and the Cailleach were on the way, began to keep his dog inside the house at night. But one night, as he slept, the dog escaped. In the morning the dog was still outside and, seeing a person pass by, barked loudly. As the bark bounced off the surrounding cliffs it echoed with such strength that the Cailleach, who was standing on the loch shore, keeled over falling down into a heap of bones. The shepherd heard the dog bark and ran out of the house and down to where the Cailleach lay. He realised she was dying and sat cradling her in his arms. She seemed to be trying to say something so he leaned in closely and she whispered: 'It was early the dog spoke, the dog spoke, it was early the dog spoke across Loch Ba.'

Note: Two stories with similar themes suggest that the Cailleach drank the waters of youth to explain her great age or perhaps that she drank the waters to become a young maiden again and then gradually aged to that of a hag until she drank of the waters again to symbolise the cycle of the seasons and of life.

Taber Cailleach

A fountain in Banffshire called the Taber Cailleach, Well of the Old Woman, became a place of pilgrimage. People would visit and leave offerings and also walk nine times around the well of virtue before walking around the menhirs that stood beside it.

Muileartaich

The water form taken by the monstrous Cailleach Bheur of Scottish Gaelic tradition was known as the Duan na Muileartaich.

Her face was blue-black, of the lustre of coal
And her bone tufted tooth was like rusted bone.
In her head was one deep pool-like eye
Swifter than a star in winter
Upon her head gnarled brushwood like the clawed old wood of the
*   aspen root.*

From Campbell, *Popular Tales of the West Highlands, Vol 3*

The Muileartaich was said to be a demon and a reptile being; a destroyer, but also a giver of life. Some stories tell of a creature that is half human and half lizard. The Scottish Muileartaich is able to raise winds and storms and one story tells how she came upon a cabin where hunters were gathered.

She asks to be allowed to sit and warm herself by the fire and then begins to swell in size. The hag demands snuff from one of the hunters, but he doesn't offer it to her, instead pointing his dirk (a long dagger) at her. She jumps and begins to choke him. The hunter's dogs spring at her and she tells him to call them off. She pulls a white hair from her head to tie them up, but the hunter uses his garter instead. The hag goes after him once the dogs are tied and says 'tighten hair', but the hunter replies with 'loosen garter'. The dogs pursue the hag and she backs out of the door. They chase her for a while until she turns and fights. The dogs return to the hunter all mangled and plucked clean of hair.

This myth is often connected with the Fians and then later Manus (Magnus Bareleg).

The name of the dauntless spectre
Was the bald-red, white-maned Muilearteach.

Her face was dark-grey of the hue of coals,
The teeth of her jaw were slanting red;
There was one flabby eye in her head
That quicker moved than lure pursuing mackerel.
Her head bristled dark and grey,
Like scrubwood before hoar-frost
James Macphearson, 1905

Cailleach Nollaigh

It was customary in Scotland at the height of winter for the head of the household to carve the face of the Cailleach Nollaigh (Christmas Old Wife) into a piece of oak. The wood represented cold and death and would be thrown into the fire on Christmas Eve to burn until it was reduced to ashes. This would ensure death would not touch the household for the coming year. It was also supposed to rid the family of any bad luck. Another Cailleach 'timber' tale tells of a log that was dragged through the village by the community, the log was named 'the Cailleach log' (obviously, what else would you call it?) but also referred to as 'the snake log'. The log was beaten by everyone and symbolically killed to represent killing all the vegetation. Everything must die first to be reborn again in the spring.

Glen Lyon

Glen Lyon is a long-enclosed valley in Scotland known for its mountain scenery and it is one of the remotest parts of the country. Deep in the glen is a small hut called a Tigh nam Bodach where a pile of stones is looked after by the locals. The stones represent the Cailleach and her family. At the beginning of spring the stones are brought out of the house and placed outside and then when winter begins the stones are returned inside. The stones are water-worn sandstone and are roughly shaped in human form. The largest stone represents the Cailleach, another is her husband Bodach and the third represents her daughter

Nighean along with a number of smaller stones believed to be her younger children.

This ritual appears to be ancient, a tradition carried on from generation to generation. It is believed to be a farming prosperity rite bringing the Cailleach out to watch over the cattle during the summer. The story goes that the Cailleach and her family were once given shelter in the glen by the locals. She was very grateful and in return left the stones with the promise that as long as they were cared for she would ensure prosperity and fertility to the land. Definitely the most well behaved house guests to have…

The Ailsa Craig

The Cailleach was wading across the ocean her apron filled with rocks when a French sailor sailed his boat through her legs. As he did so, the sail touched the Cailleach's thigh and surprised her so much so that she jumped and dropped some of her rocks which formed the island of Ailsa Craig…that would be enough to make anyone jump.

Loch Ness

This is the tale of how the Cailleach formed Loch Ness (the lake not the monster). The Cailleach looked after two wells, which she had to visit twice a day to open and then cap. She was weary of trailing between the two so she employed a young maiden to look after one of the wells; this young girl was named Nessa. One evening Nessa got held up and was late getting to the well to cap it, when she arrived she found the well overflowing; knowing the Cailleach was going to be furious Nessa ran away. The Cailleach was watching from the top of the mountain Ben Nevis and seeing what happened she placed a curse on Nessa that she had to run forever and never leave the water. Nessa became a river and a loch – thus the river Ness and Loch Ness were created.

The Corryvreckan Whirlpool

The Corryvreckan (*Coire Bhreacain* – 'the Cauldron of the Plaid') is a natural whirlpool found between Jura and Scarba in Scotland. It carries the legend of the Cailleach washing her ancient plaid of wool in the Gulf of Corryvreckan. As she washed the material her actions created a whirlpool, the noise making a great roar and bringing the first storms of winter. When the plaid was clean it turned pure white, the Cailleach spread this out to dry on the mountaintops, creating a covering of snow. A variation tells that the whirlpool was created when Breckan, the son of a Scottish king, was drowned after his boat overturned in the waves that the Cailleach had caused. Three days before she begins her reign over the winter months three of her servants stir up the water to make it ready for her. She then washes her cloak until 'the plaid of old Scotland is virgin white', creating the snow, ice and storms.

Note: This is just one of many stories about the Cailleach doing her washing and creating storms and then snow from the clean material. I am not sure what the 'washerwoman' symbolises, but perhaps it is part of her mother/creatrix role.

The Cailleach and the Well

The Cailleach was in charge of a well at the top of Ben Crauchan in Argyll, in Scotland. At sunset each day she had to cap the flowing water using a large flat stone, then at sunrise every day she removed the stone to release the water flow.

One night after a particularly long day herding her goats across the mountains she fell asleep beside the well. The water, not being capped, flowed down the hillside and broke through at the Pass of Pander creating Loch Awe, unfortunately drowning residents and cattle in the area. When she awoke and realised what had happened, she was so horrified that she instantly turned to stone.

Note: This story and variations of it are often told to explain the creation of many lakes and lochs.

Cailleach Bealtine

In some parts of the Highlands at the Bealltainn (beginning of May) festivities the 'bonnach beltine' was given out to all the men present by the master of the feast. One piece of the bannock (a flat bread) was marked and whoever got it was known as the 'Cailleach Bealtine' or the 'Bealltainn Carline' and the name tag would be held by him for the remainder of the year. He would also be dragged towards the bonfire by some of the men while the remaining people would attempt to rescue him. If he was really unlucky they would also pelt him with eggs…sounds like fun…

Note: I suspect that a big part of this play acting is to reflect that nature can be harsh.

Bannock Recipe

The bannock is a form of flat bread about the same thickness as a scone (called a biscuit in the USA) and cooked on a griddle, although it can be done in a pan or the oven. Originally it was made with oatmeal, but many variations exist. To bring abundance and luck you should eat a freshly baked bannock on Beltane morning. And because I find it terribly hard not to put at least one recipe in any of my books, here is a bannock recipe:

135g (1½ cups) oatmeal
Pinch salt
¼ teaspoon baking soda/powder
1 tablespoon butter or bacon fat/lard
115ml (½ cup) hot water

Combine the oatmeal, salt and baking soda in a bowl. Melt the butter (or fat) and add it to the oats along with the water, stir until the mixture forms a stiff dough. Turn the dough out onto a floured surface and knead for a few minutes. Divide the dough into two portions and roll each one into a ball. Using a rolling pin roll out each ball into a flat pancake that is about ¼ inch thick. Cook the bannocks on a griddle or in a pan over a medium heat until they are golden brown. Then cut each one into quarters. To serve, split each one and spread it with butter.

Cailleach Bhuain

At harvest time as the crops were gathered in each farmer would be keen not to be the last one to finish their harvesting. If they were then they had to look after and feed the Cailleach or Carline doll for the year to come. The dolly was created from the last sheaf of corn and represented the 'famine of the farm'. The corn doll was often decorated with ribbons and flowers.

In the Western Isles the last sheaf of corn to be harvested on the first farm would be made into a dolly to represent the Cailleach, the dolly was then passed from farm to farm as each one finished their ploughing until the farmer who finished completely last had the bad luck of holding onto it. The gift of the dolly was not welcome and the person delivering the Cailleach would often be chased and beaten and in some stories stripped and shaved as well…definitely not a job you would want to be picked for.

On Islay the last sheaf or Cailleach Bhuain, as it was called, was hung on the wall beside the fireplace until the time came for the farmers to plough the fields ready for the next crop. On the first day of ploughing she was taken down and split between the men of the house and the mistress. The pieces of corn were then taken to the field and fed to the horses or ploughed into the soil. This was done to ensure a good harvest and ended the power of the Cailleach over the household.

A corn doll would also often be created to represent Bride/Brighid, but she would be fashioned from the first sheaf of corn that was harvested.

Note: Perhaps the dolls were created as a representation of the importance of a good harvest and the hope for a mild winter.

Along with a big dollop of superstition about bad luck too...

Ross of Mull

The Cailleach Bheur made her home in the Ross of Mull near a point on the south west, close to the seashore. It was a wild and rocky place that was exposed to the full force of the wind and the roar of the ocean (makes you cold just to think about it). At intervals of a hundred years, when an old hag, she would immerse herself in the waters of the Loch Ba, Grulin, to regain the newness of life. If she failed to bathe in the water before the birds or beasts had greeted the day then the magic would not work. One morning just before the beasts were awake she descended the slopes to the loch and was just about to take a plunge into the waters to change her hag form into that of a maiden when she heard the distant bark of a sheep dog. The magic was broken and she dropped dead.

Note: A similar story told is in several areas. Whether the hag bathes in or drinks the water, it always has to be done before daybreak, another symbolic connection to the cycle of nature and the seasons perhaps. And always it is a dog that takes the blame...

Cailleach of Clibhrich

The Cailleach of Clibhrich used her magic of witchcraft to protect her herd of deer from hunters. However, early one morning she was milking her does at the door of her hut. One of the deer ate some blue yarn she had hanging on a nail in her house, so she removed her protection from that deer, predicting that it would be shot. And so it was.

Note: Moral of the story...don't eat blue string...perhaps it is actually a story told to warn children to do as they are told, maybe it is a tale to explain why a deer was able to be shot by a hunter when the deer were supposed to be protected by the Cailleach?

Stepping Stones

At the mouth of the Loch Etive, Connel Ferry at the Falls of Lora there are a set of stepping stones. These are often referred to as the stones that the Cailleach and her goats would walk across taking them to Benderloch and Acha-nam-ba (cow field). The circular green hollows in the fields there are called 'Cailleach Bheur's cheese vats'.

Note: A story explaining huge stones that only a giant could walk across and an explanation for hollows in the field too.

Cailleach na Mointeach

On the Isle of Lewis, in Scotland, lies a hill range that looks to be a woman lying on her back and is often said to be an earth mother or even 'the' earth mother. Locals call her 'sleeping beauty' or Cailleach na Mointeach, which translates to 'the old woman of the moors'. In the surrounding area of Callanish there are quite a few stone circles that date back 5,000 years and are positioned to link the Cailleach na Mointeach with the moon. Every eighteen and a half years or so, once a month for a few months a wonderful celestial event happens there. The moon rises over the breasts of the sleeping beauty then passes through the Callanish standing stones a few hours later.

Note: The Cailleach is ancient and this story not only tells of her age, but also suggests that it was she who created the landscape.

Finlay the Changeling

Finlay Changeling was a hunter who lived in a house in the mountains with his sister. Every morning when he left the house he would warn his sister to leave the windows shut and keep the fire going, to which she always promised. However, (as often happens in these stories) she did not do as he requested and instead opened the window to the north and shut the window to the south and let the fire go out, possibly just to annoy him because apparently they didn't get on (it's a sibling thing).

Back to Finlay...who while taking a different route one day came upon a dwelling that he had not seen before so he entered the house (no manners obviously) and saw an old woman sitting all alone on the floor. She asked him to sit down and told him that she knew all about him and that his sister was wicked and that his very own sister was willing to have him die as soon as possible. He was taken aback by this information, but the old woman confirmed it to be true. The woman continued and told him that his sister had prepared a bed on the floor of his house made with rushes that she was going to ask him to sit on that very night. The old woman advised Finlay not to adhere to her wishes, because concealed under the rushes would be a giant holding a sharp blue sword (quite how the giant was hidden under a mat of rushes we don't know). The old woman then gave exact instructions on how to avoid his death then sent him home to his sister.

On arrival at his house the sister was waiting at the door and showed him the bed she had made for him in front of the fire. Finlay kept his cool and entered the house as if nothing was wrong. He followed his usual routine, which was to wash his feet from a pot of boiling water that hung over the fire. He placed the pot of hot water onto the bed of rushes, but did not sit down. Next he ate his dinner, throwing the first bone to his dogs that lay near the bed. The three large dogs leapt upon the bed fighting over the bone, causing the pot of boiling water to fall over showering the mat with scolding water. The giant jumped up bellowing and screaming and ran from the house, followed by Finlay's sister heading towards the cave of the giants. Finlay now felt quite nervous and worried that they would return with the other giants, which I would say was very likely...but then I know how the story ends...

When the giant reached the cave, the other giants saw that he was burnt and they all volunteered to seek revenge. A young giant was selected and he headed towards Finlay's house. When he reached the door he shouted, 'Fith, foth, fugitive! there is hindrance to the poor, big stranger here. Let me in!' and he threw the door open. Finlay was ready and had already loaded his gun which he fired at the giant, which wounded him. The three dogs then leapt upon the giant and between them they slew the giant. Following the old woman's instructions Finlay immediately cut off the head, hump and neck and tied them together.

The next day Finlay headed to house of the old woman carrying with him a loaf, wine and the parts of the young giant, hopefully in separate bags...

The woman asked how he had got on and Finlay related the story and then returned home. But it was not over yet.

As night came a second giant arrived and threw open the door. Finlay was ready and shot the giant, but it made no impression so he thrust his sword into him. The dogs then joined in the fight and eventually the giant lay dead. Finlay did the same as before and cut off the head, hump and neck, taking them the following day to the old woman along with another loaf and some more wine.

He related the story to the old woman who praised his courage, but then warned him that it still wasn't over. That night the fierce grey Cailleach would arrive to avenge the death of her husband and son. She gave grave warnings and instructions to be strictly followed.

Finlay returned home and night fell. And indeed the Cailleach arrived at the door and asked most politely and meekly to be allowed in. Finlay followed the instructions given by the old woman and agreed to let her in only if she promised to be calm and polite until morning and not cause any trouble. The Cailleach promised to behave so Finlay let her in. They both sat side by side by the fire until the Cailleach moved and sat on the opposite side, shortly followed by Finlay who moved beside her.

The dogs were uneasy and prowling around the house so the

Cailleach asked Finlay to tie them up. He claimed not to have anything to tie them with so the Cailleach offered him three hairs from her head. Finlay took them, but he only pretended to tie the dogs up, getting them to lie together quietly in the corner and putting the three hairs in his pocket. Then Finlay and the Cailleach continued to sit by the fire.

Finlay suddenly noticed that the Cailleach was growing in size and remarked as much, to which she replied that it was not true. A short while later Finlay suggested again that she was growing bigger. She denied it again. Finlay wouldn't give up and tried again. The Cailleach became angry, shouting and screaming, accusing him of killing her husband and son, then she jumped up and the house shook. They met in a fight and tumbled out of the door followed by the three dogs.

They wrestled, twisting and turning for some considerable time until Finlay suddenly turned and threw the Cailleach upon her back, breaking a rib and her arm. He held her there until she offered to give him a case of gold and silver. He wouldn't accept so she added a trunk of jewellery. Still he would not give in so she also offered a watch from a king and a gold ring. Still he persisted. Next she offered a gold sword. But boy was this guy not giving up...then she offered two magical rods. Nope...not a chance. The Cailleach replied that she had no more to give. So Finlay and his three dogs killed her on the spot.

When she was dead Finlay cut out her two tusks and headed to the house of the old woman carrying them with him, telling the woman the tale and about all of the treasure that the giants had in their cave.

So the next day Finlay and the old woman headed towards the cave of giants. On the way they collected seven loads of grey heather and set them outside the cave mouth and set fire to it. The cave filled with smoke. The giant headed to the mouth of the cave and as he did so the old woman smacked him on the head with her magic wand. As the giant fell to the ground he revealed

Finlay's sister crouching behind him so Finlay fired his gun and killed her.

Then Finlay cut the head, neck and hump from the giant.

They emptied the cave of all its treasures, taking it back to the home of the old woman.

Note: Nope…I have no idea what the point of this story is either. It sets the Cailleach in a very bad light, although does follow the theme of her being a giant and also we see mention of the strength of the hairs from her head which appear in more than one story. And who was the old woman and what on earth did she do with the heads, humps and necks of the slain giants? Variations on the story tell of a young giant visiting the sister while her brother is out and also that the giants are ruled by a hag queen and also some tell that they find the sister already dead in the cave. Perhaps it is just the story of a hero or one that suggests we should listen to the wisdom of old women/elders.

The Cailleach and the Lobster

The Cailleach lived in a cabin on the summit of Cnoc an t-Sidhe. It was said that she kept great treasures in wealth hidden there. The locals were always trying to steal from her so one day she decided to go down to Scenic in Cuan Leitid and steal a lobster that she found in a pot there, she wrapped the live lobster in her apron and headed home where she put the lobster into her money box. The following day while she was out a thief crept into her house and looked everywhere for her money until he found a box under the bed. He dragged the box out and although it wasn't big it was heavy. Thinking the box was full of gold, the thief was very pleased with himself. He saw that there was a hole in the side of the box so he pushed his hand inside hoping to feel the coins. What he actually found was the sharp claws of the lobster that gripped hold of his hand. He twisted and turned trying to release the grip, but the lobster held fast. When the Cailleach returned home some time later she found the thief still being held by the lobster and killed him with her hammer.

Note: Two morals to this story, one is never to mess with the Cailleach and the second is that lobsters are obviously a good home security measure. What it actually might suggest is that the Cailleach was rich – not in the monetary sense, but in that of the nature that surrounds us. She trapped the man by using his own greed. Perhaps this story is about karma or getting what we deserve.

Carlin Maggie

Although this story refers to a witch called Carlin Maggie it does bear striking similarities to stories about the Cailleach so it may be a modernised version of a much older tale.

The Carlin Maggie stone is a 40ft natural stone column formed out of volcanic basalt and can be found above Loch Leven, in Scotland. Carlin Maggie was the head of a coven of witches who was out one day when she spotted the Devil flying towards them carrying a bag of rocks. Carlin Maggie hurled insults at the Devil who was so enraged he threw a bolt of lightning at her, which caused her to turn immediately into stone.

Note: There seem to be quite a few stories about the Devil carrying bags of rocks and, as you will see in this book, also wearing an apron full of them. Not something you would necessarily associate with the big red horned one...but maybe an attempt to Christianise some of the older folk stories of the area.

Cailleach Liath Ratharsaidh

An old Gaelic song titled Cailleach Laith Ratharsaidh (which translates as grey-haired old woman of Raasay) tells of three Hebridean Cailleachs – Raasay, Rona and Sligachan – who are very fond of fish and definitely links them to the sea. The original is obviously in Gaelic, but here is a translation:

Grey haired old woman of Raasay
Hundreds had visited her
Grey haired old woman from Raasay
And the fat old woman from Rona

The black haired woman of the cuddies
You swallowed many of them
The black haired woman for the cuddies
The messy old woman from rona

Grey haired old woman from Sligeachan
She means nothing to me
Grey haired old woman from Sligeachan
She is a big, clumsy old woman

The Cailleach in Ireland

Ireland has the legend of the Cailleach Bhearra, a sovereignty queen from West Cork. Her name also pops up in the landscape on Ceann Cailli (the hag's head) at the cliffs of Moher in County Clare and Sliabh na Cailli (the hag's mountain) in County Meath along with Slieve Gullion in County Armagh, Slieve Gallion in County Derry, Sloc na Caillagh on Rathlin, Carnacally in County Armagh – which also has a river Callan – and Caislean na Caillighe on Lough Carra, plus many more.

It is said that the Cailleach raised the mountains and hills in Ireland and placed cairns and barrow mounds upon them. This seems to reaffirm her connection with death and the under-world, but also of course with rebirth.

In Sligo, the megalithic site Carrownamaddoo (Castledargan) is also called Calliagh A Vera's House. In the mountains above Kilross, in western Tipperary, stands another stone formation often referred to as the House of the Cailleach. The Labbacallee Wedge Tomb in Cork is said to be her burial place; the name, from Irish Leabhadh Chailligh or Leaba Caillighe, means 'the Old Woman's Bed'.

La Fheill Brighde is celebrated on 1st February and is the day that the Cailleach gathers her firewood to last over the winter months. If her intention is to make the winter last a little longer she will make sure the weather on 1st February is warm and sunny so that she can gather plenty of firewood. So if the 1st February is a cold and wet day people assume that the Cailleach is already asleep and will soon run out of firewood, predicting that winter is almost over.

Calliagh Birra's House and Fionn MacCumhall

The Cailleach Bhéarra was said to live in a deep chamber under a hilltop megalith near Slieve Gullion, in Armagh. It is called

Calliagh Birra's House. The highest placed of all Irish megaliths, it sits on the southern summit of the mountain, where it aligns with solar movements. It is surrounded by kerbstones and has three flat stone basins within its chamber. The name Sliabh Gullinn means 'steep-sloped mountain'. People visited this place on Blaeberry Sunday the date of Lughnasadh. A lake near the summit is also named after the Cailleach and on the western side of Slieve Gullion the Ballykeel dolmen is known as Cathaoir na Cailli, the 'Hag's Chair'. Folklore tells that the Cailleach was the guardian of a wisdom potion that once taken would fend off age, sickness and death.

The Birra's house is also the base for the Fionn MacCumhall story – The Hunt of Slieve Cuilinn – in which a great hero suffers under the enchantment of a witch who lives in the tomb.

The story tells of Finn who was in Almhuin and saw what he believed to be a grey fawn run across the plain, he called and whistled for his hounds, but the only two that came to him were Bran and Scoelan (two of the pack). He sent them after the fawn, following closely behind them as he wasn't sure what direction the fawn had taken. He followed the hounds right to Slieve Cuilinn in Ulster. As soon as they caught sight of the fawn on the hill, it vanished, so Finn went looking to the east and he sent the hounds off to the west. Not long after Finn came to a lake and there on the banks sat a young girl with the most beautiful gold coloured hair he had ever seen and with skin as white as lime (limestone not lime citrus fruits obviously). The girl seemed very sad and downhearted. Finn asked if she had seen his hounds pass her by to which she replied that she had not. Finn asked the girl what was troubling her and she told him she had lost a red gold ring from her hand into the waters of the lake. She ended her sentence with a command that Finn was under a bond to bring it back for her out of the lake. Well that boy stripped off so quickly and was no sooner in the lake, swimming three times round it searching every part until he found the ring, which he brought back and handed to the girl. As soon as she had the ring in her hand...she leapt into the water and vanished (well that's gratitude for you).

As Finn stepped out of the water and onto the bank he found he was struggling to walk. Feeling stiff and old he realised he was exactly that...he had transformed into an old, weak, withered white-haired man.

The rest of his men started to get a bit worried about his whereabouts so they set out to look for Finn and at last came to Slieve Cuilinn where they saw an old man sitting by the lake. They asked him if he had seen a young man and his hounds. Finn recounted the whole tale to them and realising it really was their leader they cried in sorrow. Loch Doghra, which is where they were, is called 'the Lake of Sorrow'.

So where does the Cailleach feature in this story? Well...the guys dig a passage into the tomb of Caillagh Berra's house and steal the youth potion from her. As soon as Finn drinks the magic liquid he returns to his usual appearance...all but his hair, which stayed snow white.

Note: It seems that this story can be dated back to the 3rd century CE and the earliest references to the Fenian stories can be found in texts from the 8th and 9th centuries although some are from the 12th century. But it does show the use of the Cailleach's magic youth potion.

The Red Lake

A north Irish tale tells that the Cailleach was killed then mutilated by the Fianna (warrior bands). As her slain body lay still a long hairy worm crept out from one of her thigh bones (can I just say ewww!). A warning was given to the warriors by a dwarf that if this worm found water to drink it would destroy the whole world. One of the impulsive Fiannas called Conan lifted the worm with the tip of his spear and flung it into the Lough Derg saying, 'There is water enough for you.' The worm obviously enjoyed the very long drink and became an 'enormous beast' that overran the country causing destruction and chaos along with eating anyone that it found in its path. The creature did, however, have a weak spot – a mole on its left side. One of the warriors, Fionn, discovered this and wounded it there, the blood turning the water red, which is where the name Lough Derg came from, meaning 'red lake'.

Note: There are a few tales that seem to suggest the Cailleach was a monster or a beast, especially one that lived under water. I have even read suggestions that she may have been able to shape-shift into a dragon too, but that one I am not so sure about…let's just put that down to 'creative fantasy'. Does this story tell of brave warriors or stupid ones? It does seem to suggest a rebirth or at least a life from death tale, at least for the worm anyway. And of course it explains why the water in the lake is red…

The Shower of Stones

Two Cailleachs who both lived in Magh Cuilinn in Ireland got into an argument. What they were in disagreement about we don't know, but suffice to say it got very heated to the point that they agreed to hold a stone throwing contest and when I say stones I don't mean pebbles, we are talking huge great big boulders because giants wouldn't use anything else. They went to the top of Poll Mountain and stood a distance apart, each on a separate hilltop, at which point they both collected huge piles of ammunition in the form of rocks.

At dawn the next day they took their positions and started throwing rocks at each other. It was not a pretty sight, rocks flew and each of them ended up battered, bruised and bleeding. As the contest continued one of the Cailleachs (the Cailleach Bearra) started throwing her rocks over the head of the other Cailleach (her name does not seem to have been recorded) so that they landed beyond her. The other Cailleach took her chance and gathered up all her remaining rocks and threw them in quick succession causing the Cailleach Bearra much pain. But soon the Cailleach's rocks were all gone while the Cailleach Bearra was left with a huge pile of stones. The Cailleach Bearra then proceeded to bombard the other Cailleach with all her ammo, reducing her to a pile of bones. The rocks have long since gone and the only reminder left today is a cairn where the Cailleach fell.

Note: This story is only one that tells of the Cailleach as being more than one person, the title perhaps for several supernatural deities. It is, however, another 'piles of rock' story explaining how the Cailleach shaped the landscape.

Shanven

In Altagore, county Antrim, stood a stone referred to by locals as the Shanven 'old woman'. It was considered sacred and people would leave offerings of food and drink there. One tale tells of a mason who chose to ignore the powers of the stone and moved it to use as a gate post...the very next morning it had returned to its original place.

Slyne Head

The Cailleach was in a boat on the sea in the area of Slyne Head together with her children, it was cold and dark and absolutely freezing. The children were so cold the chill went through to the marrow in their bones. To keep them warm the Cailleach instructed the children to bail the water from the sea into the boat...and then back out again. Thus making them move about and keep them warm until morning. Definitely the wisdom of a mother looking after her children.

Witch's Stone

There is a bullan (rock basin) near Antrim that is known as the Witch's Stone. The story tells that when the Cailleach had finished building the Round Tower she leaped off the top and landed onto this stone leaving marks in the rock from her elbow and her knee.

Lake of Two Geese

The Cailleach was apparently so tall that she was able to wade comfortably in all of Ireland's rivers and lakes, but she drowned while crossing the deepest loch in Sligo, the Lake of Two Geese. There is a rumour that this lake has an underground outlet and a monster that guards treasure in the depths.

Note: Several tales tell of the height of the Cailleach and her ability to wade through deep rivers and lakes, but this one also mentions a water monster, which is also a bit of a reoccurring theme.

Sliabh na Caillighe

The megalithic chambers of Loughcrew stand atop a low range of mountains in eastern Meath, Slilabh na Caillighe, 'the old woman's mountains'.

Jonathan swift wrote in 1710:

Determined now her tomb to build,
Her ample skirt with stones she filled,
And dropped a heap on Carnmore;
Then stepped one thousand yards, to Loar,
And dropped another goodly heap;
And then with one prodigious leap
Gained Carnbeg; and on its height
Displayed the wonders of her might.
And when approached death's awful doom,
Her chair was placed within the womb
Of hills whose tops with heather bloom
The three hilltops are covered in cairns (passage graves or womb tombs).

Remains of cremations have been found on the flat stone basins and under the soil inside the Loughcrew passages and it seems they may have been collective burial sites. This site also offers solar alignments and was probably used for ceremonies too. The view from the top of the hills covers more than half the counties of Ireland. The cairns themselves are covered in quartz pebbles, which makes a beautiful sight when the sun hits them. Originally covered by mounds, some of these megalithic stone chambers still are and some are surrounded by huge kerbstones. You enter through passageways lined with stones, which also include engravings of mystical symbols such as circles, vulvas, cup marks and sun signs.

Some of the cairns have a back stone that faces the entryway engraved with elaborate carvings that at certain times of the year (the equinoxes for instance) are lit up by the sun. The main cairn has a back stone covered in intricate designs of circles, spirals and vulvas and a standing stone in the central chamber made from blue limestone, called The Whispering Stone. It receives the rays of sunlight at set calendar intervals.

Note: The mountain range is called 'the old woman's mountains' and must have some sort of connection to the Cailleach especially with all the stone chambers. It sounds like a truly magical place.

The Hag's Chair

The Hag's Chair at Cairn T faces north, looking across the countryside. It is a 10ft by 6ft stone seat engraved with concentric circles, portals, cupules, cup-and-ring marks, triangles, and what could possibly be a snake. Most of the symbols have greatly eroded and very few of the markings remained visible sadly. Folklore says that the Cailleach looked out over her domain from this chair where she watched the stars. Local traditions say that a visitor, when seated on the chair, will be granted a single wish.

Garavogue is the name given to the Cailleach in the stories

about Loughcrew. Megalithic tradition in Sligo also names the Cailleach Garavogue (Gharbhóg) who shares her name with a river in that county. In a later telling of the Loughcrew story, the Cailleach Bhéarra came there from the north to perform a magical act that would give her great power. She filled her apron with stones, dropping a cairn on Carnbane; then jumped a mile to Slieve-na-cally (Hag's Mountain) to drop another, and on to the next hill, where she let another stone fall. On her fourth and final leap she slipped and fell to her death.

Note: Yep more stones in the apron stories, but in this one there isn't a happy ending. The death of the Cailleach is perhaps symbolic of the cycle of life that she is so often linked with.

The Hag of Beara

Legend has it that this rock, which rises above Coulagh Bay, represents the fossilised remains of the face of the Cailleach Beara awaiting her husband Manannan, God of the Sea, to return to her. Visitors leave coins, trinkets and all sorts of small offerings, on and around the rock.

There are several other legends. One says that the Cailleach Beara stole a Bible from the Catholic cleric Caitighearn. In order to recover his book Caitighearn hit the Cailleach Beara with his staff instantly turning her to stone. This has most definitely got to be a story created once Christianity arrived and the attempt to beat down the pagan beliefs.

Then there is the story that the Cailleach Beara was visited by a monk who asked about her great age. She replied that each year she killed a bullock and threw a bone from it into the loft of her house. The monk sent his servant up into the loft to count the bones, but it took so long that the monk lost patience.

When asked about her age on another occasion, the Cailleach Beara replied that the top of her head had never seen the air, the sole of her foot had never touched the ground, she never ate unless she was hungry and she never stayed in bed after waking up.

Another tale tells that the Cailleach had two sister hags, one lived on the Kerry peninsula of Dingle and the other over in Iveragh. When she fell on hard times the Dingle hag decided to help her by presenting her with an extra island. The Dingle hag put a straw rope around the island and started to drag it to the south, but it split in two and the straw broke at the Iveragh peninsula and so the islands of Scariff and Deenish came into being.

Then there is the tale of the Cailleach and her extremely good eyesight. The Iveragh hag was working on her house at Bolus one day when she heard a shout outside. It was the hag of Beare (the Cailleach) warning her that her cow had gone into the cornfield beside her house. The hag of Beare had seen this happening from 20 miles away across the sea.

The hag of Beare is also said to have owned a great bull called the Tarbh Conraidh and every cow who heard his bellow calved within a year. The bull once swam after a cow across a creek; the hag jumped in after him and struck him with her rod, which turned him into a rock.

In Connacht, north Leinster and south Ulster, in Ireland, the hag of Beara is associated with corn and harvesting. It is said that the Cailleach Bhearra had a huge cornfield and that she issued a challenge to everyone for a reaping competition against her. She beat every single man and cut the legs from under each one with a stroke of her sickle. However, one clever man discovered that she had a magical black beetle hidden in the handle of her sickle that was helping her win. He killed the beetle and defeated her. In return for winning, the hag shared her wisdom with him, telling of her great age and gave him some good farming advice, advising how she sowed in late winter and harvested the green corn before the autumn winds arrived. The corn was known as coerce na bhFaoilli (the oats of February) and was much better than the mixed oats and crops sown in March or April. She also showed him a more efficient method of threshing using a flail made from holly and hazel.

The Lament of the Old Woman of Beare

There is a poem thought to date back to around 800CE called The Lament of the Old Woman of Beare where she calls herself Buí and talks about her youth and the fun she had, mourning now that she is an old hag.

Ebb-tide has come to me as to the sea;
old age makes me yellow;
though I may grieve there at,
it approaches its food joyfully.

I am Buí, the Old Woman of Beare;
I used to wear a smock that was ever-renewed;
today it has befallen me, by reason of my mean estate,
that I could not have even a cast-off smock to wear.

It is riches
you love, and not people;
as for us, when we lived,
it was people we loved.

Beloved were the people
whose plains we ride over;
well did we fare among them,
and they boasted little thereafter.

Today indeed you are good at claiming,
and you are not lavish in granting the claim;
though it is little you bestow,
greatly do you boast.

Swift chariots

and steeds that carried off the prize,
there has been, for a time, a flood of them:
a blessing on the King who has granted them!

My body, full of bitterness,
seeks to go to a dwelling where it is known:
when the Son of God deems it time,
let Him come to carry off His deposit.

When my arms are seen,
all bony and thin!
The craft they used to practise was pleasant:
they used to be about glorious kings.

When my arms are seen,
all bony and thin,
they are not, I declare,
worth raising around comely youths.

The maidens are joyful
when they reach May-day;
grief is more fitting for me:
I am not only miserable, but an old woman.

I speak no honied words;
no wethers are killed for my wedding;
my hair is scant and grey;
to have a mean veil over it causes no regret.

To have a white veil
on my head causes me no grief;
many coverings of every hue
were on my head as we drank good ale.

I envy no one old,
excepting only Feimen:
as for me, I have worn an old person's garb;
Feimen's crop is still yellow.

The Stone of the Kings in Feimen,
Rónán's Dwelling in Bregun,
it is long since storms first reached their cheeks;
but they are not old and withered.

I know what they are doing:
they row and row off;
the reeds of Ath Alma,
cold is the dwelling in which they sleep.

Alack-a-day
that I sail not over youth's sea!
Many years of my beauty are departed,
for my wantonness has been used up.

Alack the day
Now, whatever haze there be,
I must take my garment even when the sun shines:
age is upon me; I myself recognise it.

Summer of youth in which we have been
I spent with its autumn;
winter of age which overwhelms everyone,
its first months have come to me.

I have spent my youth in the beginning;
I am satisfied with my decision:
though my leap beyond the wall had been small,
the cloak would not have been still new.

Delightful is the cloak of green
which my King has spread over Drumain.
Noble is He who fulls it:
He has bestowed wool on it after rough cloth.

I am cold indeed;
every acorn is doomed to decay.
After feasting by bright candles
to be in the darkness of an oratory!

I have had my day with kings,
drinking mead and wine;
now I drink whey-and-water
among shrivelled old hags.

May a little cup of whey be my ale;
may whatever may vex me be God's will;
praying to thee, O living God,
may I give...against anger.

I see on my cloak the stains of age;
my reason has begun to deceive me;
grey is the hair which grows through my skin;
the decay of an ancient tree is like this.

My right eye has been taken from me
to be sold for a land that will be forever mine;
the left eye has been taken also,
to make my claim to that land more secure.

There are three floods
which approach the fort of Ard Ruide:
a flood of warriors, a flood of steeds,
a flood of the greyhounds owned by Lugaid's sons.

The flood-wave
and that of swift ebb:
what the flood-wave brings you
the ebb-wave carries out of your hand.

The flood-wave
and that second wave which is ebb:
all have come to me
so that I know how to recognise them.

The flood-wave,
may the silence of my cellar not come to it!
Though my retinue in the dark be great,
a hand was laid on them all.

Had the Son of Mary
the knowledge that He would be beneath the house-pole of my
cellar!
Though I have practised liberality in no other way,
I have never said 'No' to anyone.

It is wholly sad
(man is the basest of creatures)
that ebb was not seen
as the flood had been.

My flood
has guarded well that which was deposited with me.
Jesus, Son of Mary, has saved it
till ebb so that I am not sad.

It is well for an island of the great sea:
flood comes to it after its ebb;
as for me, I expect

no flood after ebb to come to me.

Today there is scarcely
a dwelling-place I could recognise;
what was in flood
is all ebbing.

Princess Beara

A story tells of a Spanish princess named Beara who was advised to travel to the river Eibhear on a certain night and seek out a salmon dressed in colourful garments (like you do...) that lived there. On that night she was told she would meet her future husband. So she did this and ended up eloping with Eoghan Mo'r of Magh Nuadat. They set sail together for Ireland and upon their arrival landed on the north side of Bantry Bay. Eoghan named the peninsula after his wife, Beara.

The Nine Hostages

Niall and his eight brothers encountered an old hag woman who captured them and held them hostage until one of them agreed to kiss her. Only Niall and one of his brothers Fergus resisted the urge to kill her because of her ugliness. Fergus kissed the hag on the cheek and was rewarded with sovereignty over all of Ireland at which point the hag then turned into a beautiful young woman.

The Sons of Eochaid Mugmedn

A variation on the Nine Hostages story. Five brothers, all the sons of Eochaid Mugmedn, set out on a manhood quest. They got lost and one was sent to find drinking water. When he stumbled upon a well he found that it was guarded by a frightening black hag. She promised to let him draw water from the well if he kissed her first. He refused, but his brother Niall did the deed. She then transformed into a beautiful woman who gave him the title King of Tara and vowed that all his descendants would rule after him.

Note: The sovereignty stories seem to tell of tests for a new king. By appearing in her most repulsive guise the Cailleach tests the potential new king for his true worth. If he is not swayed by appearance and can see beyond the exterior and is willing to put aside his feelings to help save those trapped with him then that makes him worthy. There is a recurring theme with the ugly old hag demanding sometimes as little as a peck on the cheek other times much, much more...but each time the man who is brave enough is rewarded usually with sovereignty of some kind and nearly always the hag turning into a fair maiden. This definitely shows the Cailleach connection to the land and the monarchy as well as the transition from hag into maiden like the seasons.

The Hag's Bed

The wedge tomb at Labbacallee is the largest of all the Irish wedge tombs, known as Leaba Caillighe, which translates to 'the bed of the witch' (or hag). The tomb is associated with the Cailleach Bhearra. It is covered by three huge capstones and the tomb has three large buttress stones at the rear set parallel to the gallery. The tomb is also triple walled with large stones. The front of the tomb has the remains of a large portico wider than the actual gallery. Around the southern side of the tomb are the remains of the kerbing of the cairn that once covered this huge megalithic monument. Also to the south was at one time a small round modern cairn, but this cairn has now been removed.

The local tale associated with this tomb is that of the Cailleach Bhearra and her hostility towards her husband, the druid Mogh Ruith. The Cailleach was cross with her husband because he removed the dew from the grass before she was able to. She was with child and he felt bad so he told her to go to see her sister on the hill above Burtroche near Ballyhooly. When she had gone he put his coat on the big stone and went across the stream. On her return she thought the coat was her husband so she struck the stone with her sword. Realising it was just a stone she sought her husband out, followed him and threw the stone at him as he was crossing the river, it hit him and he was drowned. He is said to be buried in a nearby cairn Thierna. Not much marital bliss there then…

County Mayo

A story from County Mayo tells of the Cailleach Beara who was building a tower to reach the skies when she was interrupted by a young boy who made a rude comment about her bottom. She was so incensed that she jumped down and abandoned her building, leaving just the tower standing and making marks in the rocks below it from her knees as she landed.

Note: Sound familiar? Another story attributing the Cailleach's knees to explain the landscape.

The Cailleach and the Fianna

The Cailleach turned up at the house of the leader of a group of Fianna (warrior bands, often young aristocrats who had not yet come into their inheritance). She pleaded with him that she might be allowed in to sit by the fire and rest for a while. Once he had taken himself off to bed the hag quietly climbed in with him. He was extremely accommodating and let her stay, but put a fold of bed linen between them (such a gentleman). When he awoke the next morning he was extremely surprised to find that the old hag he went to bed with had miraculously transformed into a beautiful young maiden.

Note: Telling the story of winter turning into spring, the transition of crone into the maiden and the surprising willingness of young men to unquestionably allow old hags into their beds…

Fintan the Wise

Fintan mac Bochra known as Fintan the Wise was a seer who accompanied Noah's granddaughter Cessair to Ireland before the deluge. Unfortunately his wives (he had several) were drowned in the flood, but he survived after shape-shifting into a salmon. Legend tells that he lived for 5,500 years after the deluge, becoming an advisor to the kings of Ireland. He held the knowledge of all Ireland and its history, the job that was also held by a hawk – the Hawk of Achill that was born at the same time as him. Apparently once Ireland was converted to Christianity and sometime during the 5th century, Fintan and the Hawk decided to leave the land of the living. Fintan, the Hawk and the Cailleach had a discussion as they were about to depart, both Fintan and the Hawk agreed that she had outlived them, both saying, 'Are you are the one, the grandmother who ate the apples in the beginning?'

Note: An interesting story that tells of the great age of the Cailleach.

Cailleach An Airgid

This is an old Irish folk song from Connemara called Cailleach An Airgid, which translates as 'she's your granny' and which is translated here into English:

Chorus:
She is your granny, she is your granny
She's your granny, the hag with the money
She's your granny, from Iorras Mhór (Nishmore)
And she would put coaches
On the roads of Cois Farraige

If you'd see the steam
Going past Toin Ui Loin'
And the wheels turning speedily out from her flanks

She'd scatter the stour nine times to the rear
But she'd never keep pace
With the hag with the money

Do you reckon he'd marry, do you reckon he'd marry
Do you reckon he'd marry the hag with the money?
I know he'll not marry, I know he'll not marry
'Cause he's too young and he'll squander the money

We'll soon have a wedding, we'll soon have a wedding
We'll soon have a wedding, by two in the village
We'll soon have a wedding, we'll soon have a wedding
Between Sean Seamais Mhoir and Maire Ni Chathasaigh

I would go courting Oighrig
To make love to the maiden
I would go seeking your kindness
Though the night be freezing

How little do I like what I see
Women who eat and then tell tales
That came easily to my woman
They gave her the butter while still young

The Cailleach and Brighid

There are different versions of the Cailleach/Bride story and I present two of them here although the story does seem to be relatively modern (Mackenzie includes the story in his book *Wonder Tales from Scottish Myth and Legend* – 1917). The Cailleach and the Bride is probably the most well known story about the Cailleach and her connection with the goddess Brighid, but in some tales it is suggested that they are one and the same, the Cailleach turning into the goddess Bride/Brighid at Imbolc and then reverting back to her hag guise of the Cailleach at Samhain. My personal thoughts are that they remain very much two separate deities, but it is up to you to make that decision.

The Cailleach and the Well of Youth

On the eve of Imbolc the Cailleach goes on a journey to a magical island which has in its centre a woodland. Inside the woods the Cailleach finds a well of youth. At the first glimpse of dawn she drinks from the fresh water that bubbles from a crevice in the rocks and is completely transformed from the old hag Cailleach into a young and beautiful maiden, the goddess Bride who carries a wand that turns the bare earth and naked trees into flourishing greenery again. And presumably the reverse happens at Samhain to turn Bride back into the Cailleach.

The Cailleach and the Bride

The connection with the goddess Brighid is told in the story The Cailleach and the Bride. The Cailleach Beira holds the maiden Bride (Brighid) captive in the mountains, often noted as being the mountain Ben Nevis. She basically kept Bride as a slave making her do all the work. The Cailleach gave Bride a dirty brown fleece to wash, insisting she wash it clean in the stream until it was pure white. Bride washed and washed that fleece over and over, but it stayed brown. One day an old man passed by and asked what she was doing. After she had explained, he took the fleece and tapped it three times; on the third tap it turned white. He also gave her a bunch of snowdrops telling Bride to give the Cailleach the flowers and to tell her that they came from the green rustling fir woods and to also let her know that the cress was beginning to grow by the stream and the grass in the fields was starting to shoot.

When Bride returned to the Cailleach she gave her the snowdrops and the message (seems the old man was in fact Father Winter). The Cailleach was furious. The Cailleach called her eight hag servants and they all set out to each of the directions to cover the land with frost and to kill all the new plant growth (never upset the Cailleach...).

The Cailleach was keeping Bride a prisoner to keep her away from her son Angus who had fallen in love with Bride. The longer she kept Bride away from Angus the longer she could rule as Queen of Winter.

Angus was impatient and even though it was only February he borrowed three days from August and cast a spell on the land to bring good weather. He spent those three days searching for Bride in vain and on the third day the Cailleach caused a storm to send Angus back. So when it rains on your summer holiday in August you know who to hold responsible...

Angus was not beaten and set out to search again until he finally found Bride on the first day of spring – Brides' Day. They found some faeries who took them to the faery court where they were married and in celebration Angus cast spells of growth across the land. The Cailleach was beyond furious (seems to be a habit with her) and countered his spells with a ground frost. The battle between them continued until the Cailleach borrowed three days from winter to cause havoc, freezing winds and cold weather, and then she was done. At the end of the spring the Cailleach drank the healing, restoring waters of youth.

Note: This echoes many stories where the Cailleach transforms from crone to maiden to symbolise the changing of the seasons. This also tells the story of the ups and downs of our spring weather.

On that day which is of equal length with the night, Angus came to Scotland with Bride, and they were hailed as king and queen of the unseen beings. They rode from south to north in the morning and forenoon, and from north to south in the afternoon and evening. A gentle wind went with them, blowing towards the north from dawn till midday, and towards the south from midday till sunset.

It was on that day that Bride dipped her fair white hands in the high rivers and lochs which still retained ice. When she did so, the Ice Hag fell into a deep sleep from which she could not awake until summer and autumn were over and past.

Mackenzie, 1917

The Cailleach on the Isle of Man

The Cailleach ny Groamagh or Caillagh ny Gueshag as she is called on the Isle of Man is said to foretell the weather. On 1st February if it is good weather she comes out in her guise as a winter and storm spirit to enjoy the sunshine…this predicts bad luck for the year to come.

Note: Another weather story connected to the beginning of spring, reminds me of the American tradition of Groundhog Day!

The Cailleach in England

There are some folk stories around parts of England that refer to a giantess. Although there doesn't seem to be any specific mention of the Cailleach by name, a lot of the stories refer to an old woman, hag or old witch. I have related some of them here for you to draw your own conclusions (also see Black Annis).

Standing Stones

It seems that a lot of standing stones in England (and across the globe) are often referred to as 'old woman', most of them have little or no legends or stories to go with them, but maybe they do refer to the ancient goddess, the Cailleach, when she is turned to stone? The Old Woman stone on Bamford Moor, Derbyshire, and another Old Woman stone in Cornholme, West Yorkshire, are just two examples.

There is also a huge stone on the western boundary of Pevensey, in Sussex. Folklore says that an old woman was bringing the stone as her contribution to the foundations of Pevensey Castle. On the way her apron strings broke and the stone dropped so she left it there. Another apron string story...

In the North of England in the country of Cumbria sits a huge 350ft diameter stone circle consisting of 69 stones, the tallest of which is about 12ft high and carved with symbols. The four corners face the points of the compass. The stones date back to around 1500BC. The largest stone is called Long Meg, who was said to be a witch who with her daughters was turned to stone for cursing and dancing on the Sabbath (apparently partying on the Sabbath is a bit of a no no). The circle is said to be filled with magic and you are supposedly not able to count the same number of stones twice.

The Witch of Wookey Hole

Possibly one of the most well known witches in England is the Witch of Wookey Hole. The site is a series of limestone caverns in the village of Wookey Hole on the edge of the Mendip Hills in Somerset. The name Wookey Hole translates from Celtic and Anglo Saxon as 'cave, cave' – you can't get clearer than that… The caves have apparently been used by man for around 45,000 years, as tools and fossilised animal remains have been unearthed there from the Palaeolithic period and it seems it continued to be used right through the Stone Age and Iron Age and well into Roman times in Britain.

The Witch in question is a roughly human-shaped stalagmite in one of the caves and the legend has it that during the Dark Ages an old woman lived in the cave with her dog and herd of goats. All of the mishaps and illnesses in the nearby village were blamed on her. The locals believed she was a witch who spent her time cursing them. Well, the villagers understandably got a bit fed up and called in assistance from an abbot in nearby Glastonbury Abbey. He sent a monk called Father Bernard to deal with the old woman. The monk entered the cave carrying a Bible and a candle and as his sight adjusted to the dim light in the cave he could just make out the old woman bending over her cooking pot. He tried to talk to her, but her response was to shout and scream curses and hexes at him as she fled deeper into the cave and down a narrow passageway called Hell's Ladder. The monk undeterred followed and caught up with her in the dark inner cavern. Obviously being a quick thinker Father Bernard scooped up a handful of water from the river that ran through the cavern, said a few words over it as a blessing and threw the water at the old woman. She was turned into stone on the spot and that is where her stone figure stands to this day.

Note: Although there is no obvious connection to the Cailleach in this story it is reminiscent of lots of old woman/witch stories and perhaps stems originally from tales of the crone goddess. It is also another story where Christianity triumphs over witches.

The Rollright Stones

The Rollright stones are an ancient site on the Oxfordshire/ Warwickshire border in England and consist of three main elements – the King's Men stone circle, the King Stone and the Whispering Knights. I have no idea whether these stones could be linked to the Cailleach, but there is the witch connection and it is an ancient site, perhaps it is? Many stone circles are said to be the images of revellers who were turned to stone by the hand of God or the Devil for wicked behaviour (such as dancing) on the Sabbath. They may have originated when Christianity was trying to win over the pagans or maybe later by the Puritans, but I do wonder if the stories had their roots before then.

The Rollright story was printed in 1586 and goes like this: A king on his way to conquer all of England got as far as the Rollrights when he encountered an old witch and she challenged him. Well he wasn't having any of that nonsense and as he strode onwards, the ground rose up before him in a long mound (often called the Arch Druid's Barrow). The witch laughed and the king and all his men were turned to stone. The witch then turned herself into an elder tree (a tree that has strong connections to the Cailleach).

The stones are also connected to the world of Faerie (as is the Cailleach) with caves underneath the stone circle that house the faerie folk.

The Petrifying Well

There is an ancient well in Knaresborough, Yorkshire, that used to be called the Dropping Well, but is now known as the Petrifying Well because that's exactly what it does, due to a naturally high mineral content in the water it literally petrifies items that fall into it (although not instantly, it does take a little time). People believed the well was magic and that if you touched the waters you would be turned into stone. Also to the side of the well is what looks like a giant's skull in the rock.

Note: Although a very tenuous link to the Cailleach, wells were sacred to her and with the magical powers of turning items to stone and the giant's skull beside it...maybe?

Kit's Coty

In Aylesford, in Kent, you will find two megalithic dolmen burial chambers, Kit's Coty House and Little Kit's Coty House. The origins of the names are unknown, but they are long barrows that were probably constructed during the early Neolithic period. The stones were said to have been put in place by a group of four witches.

Great Four Stones

The main great stone sits on the boundary between Yorkshire and Lancashire, just inside Yorkshire at Lowgill. Originally the great stone was accompanied by three others, making a stone circle. Unfortunately the other three were broken up many years ago. The story was that the Devil created the circle of stones when he dropped the rocks from his apron (yep another broken apron string story) another story tells that the three missing stones were stolen by the Devil some time later. Yet another tale attributes the rocks to the giant Finn McCool who threw them across the Irish sea in a fit of anger.

Note: More apron string stories and the Devil and even Finn McCool, so maybe there is a Cailleach connection here?

Spinsters Rock

Just outside Chagford in the county of Devon you will find another Neolithic dolmen (sometimes called a cromlech). The legend tells of three spinsters who with time to kill before breakfast one morning while waiting for their woollen cloth to be collected, decided to occupy themselves by balancing a few large stones to create the rock shape we see today. Obviously there wasn't much entertainment in those days…

The Devil's Chair

In the hills south of Pontesbury, in Shropshire, lies a ridge of Stiperstones and the most well known of these is called the Devil's Chair, it is the highest point and the most imposing of the outcrops. Local legend tells that the Devil was travelling across Britain from Ireland carrying a load of rocks in his apron when he felt tired and decided to rest awhile. The stones were apparently going to be used to fill a valley on the other side of the Stiperstones called Hell's Gutter. However, as the Devil arose from the ground after resting, his apron string broke and the rocks tumbled out. Being kinda lazy the Devil decided not to bother to pick the stones up and instead left them scattered all over the ridge with some of them forming the shape of a chair. It is said that when you visit on a hot day you can smell the brimstone coming from the stones…

The legend doesn't end there because on the longest night of the year the Devil arrives to sit on his chair and puts out a call to all the local evil spirits and wicked witches (such a stereotype) and they then pick their king for the year ahead.

Note: As the Devil didn't appear until Christianity arrived this is possibly another story based on an earlier tale of a supernatural being such as the Cailleach, especially as the story mirrors a lot of her tales and of course those apron strings again…

Old Woman's Well

In a directory for North Yorkshire written in 1928 by A H Smith, talking about the etymology of 'Carling Howe' at Guisborough, in North Yorkshire, there are references to a Kerlinghou, which translates as 'the old woman's mound' and also references made in a 12th century article the Guisborough Cartulary of a Kerlingkelde, which means 'old woman's well'. The word 'hou' often referred to a prehistoric tomb so this was perhaps an old woman's grave. The old woman is assumed to be the Cailleach.

Wade's Wife's Causeway

There is a long stretch of ancient trackway that runs between Malton and Whitby, in Yorkshire (it is about 25 miles long). It is often credited as a Roman-built road, but the actual date of construction has been the subject of much debate. It doesn't really seem to fit the typical profile of a Roman road and the suggestion is that it may even be part of a Neolithic boundary of some sort. Anyway...there are variations on the myth that surround it. One says that a giant named Wade (Wayland or even Woden/Odin maybe?) was in dispute with another giant so he scooped out a handful of earth to throw at him; this great scoop created the gorge known as the Hole of Horcum. The lump of earth missed the giant and where it landed created the hill known as Blakey Topping. The trackway between the two is the Old Wives Way or Wade's Wife's Causeway. Perhaps the dispute was about his wife? There is also an ancient sacred spring and well not far away called the Old Wives Well.

Another version of the tale tells of Wade's wife who was named Bell, also a giant. They would herd their cows every day onto the moor and built the causeway to make the journey easier. Bell created the causeway by carrying rocks in her apron, unfortunately after a couple of trips the apron strings broke leaving piles of stones across the moor.

There is also a tall standing stone in the North York Moors National Park known as Wade's Stone and said to be named after the giant. Not far from the first standing stone is another that is said to mark his grave. Wade and his wife Bell apparently lived in a castle in Lythe, keeping their cattle on the moors.

Note: Perhaps there is a Cailleach connection here. The story of the apron strings crops up again and the creation of landscapes.

Lady of the Beasts

As Lady of the Beasts the Cailleach performs her duties as guardian to all creatures and keeps the balance of nature. She works her powers with the elements and sings magical songs to charm the beasts.

There is a very strong connection between the Cailleach and deer, but also wild boar, pigs, cattle, goats and wolves. The Cailleach oidhche, or owl, is sacred to her and associated with the underworld, magic, death and the spirit world. Although she also has a reputation of shape-shifting particularly into a giant bird (some say a heron).

Gaelic tales tell of the winter goddess riding through the sky on the back of a wolf. This may be connected to the old Gaelic name for the month of January, which is 'Faoilleach' or 'wolf month'.

She herds the cattle and goats and milks them and often protects them and herds of deer against hunters.

Other stories tell of her as a fishing goddess bringing protection to the wildlife found in wells and streams.

It is said that her fearful appearance actually scares the animals into hiding over the harsh cold winter months, thus keeping them safe until the spring.

She seems to favour cattle in Ireland and deer in Scotland. Folk stories say that the Cailleach wanders with her herd of deer along the beaches at night where they devour the 'sea-tangle'.

The Cailleach and the Hunters

This story tells of two young hunters who were out in the woods to take down a large stag. They met the Cailleach in the forest and she directed them to the location of the stag, but she also advised them to give a blessing to the stag and the earth after the kill. The hunters found the stag and killed it then proceeded to drag the heavy beast home, which was quite a long journey and took some time. Once they reached their home they left the stag outside and went into the house to tell their father of their kill. They came back outside to find the stag gone. The father asked if they blessed the stag as the Cailleach had advised, to which they replied that they had not. The father responded with: 'If you don't bless the animal then the faeries have a right to take their share!'

The Cailleach and Deer

A more recent story, well 1773 to be exact, tells of two hunters who set out from Braemar (in Scotland) to search for red deer.

Heading to the forest of Atholl they were hit with a snowstorm coming from the north although it soon cleared. When they reached the forest they shot and wounded a hind. They were following her trail (from the drops of blood in the snow) when the storm hit again, but much harder. They found shelter in some rocks and settled down to wait out the night. In the morning the storm had cleared a little although the visibility was very limited and there was a strong wind. Forgetting the deer they focussed on surviving and finding their way home. They set out but the storm played havoc with their idea of what direction they were heading, so instead of heading south they ended up veering to the west.

Night arrived again and their provisions were running very low. As they sought shelter for the night they spotted an old sheiling bothy (shepherd/cattle herder summer shelter) ahead of them so they made their way towards it. As they arrived at the shelter, much to their surprise the door swung open and there stood an old hag woman, she told them she was expecting their arrival and invited them in. Inside the woman had a hot supper ready for them and beds made up. As the old woman poured out bowls of soup she sang a song in a language they didn't know.

Although they were cold and hungry they had a strange

feeling that something uncanny was happening and they hesitated to eat. The old woman told them she had power over the weather and held up a rope with three knots in it. As she did so she explained that if she untied the first knot a fair wind would blow, the second would create a stronger blast of wind and the third would unleash an horrendous storm.

She went on to say:

'As I sit on my throne of Cairn-Gower, on the tap o Ben-y-Gloe. Weel did ye ken my pouer the day, when the wind was cauld and dedly, and all was dimmed in snaw – and ye see that ye was expectit here, and ye hae brought nae venison; but if ye mean to thrive, ye maun place a fat hart, or a yeld [barren] hind in the braes o' Atholl, by Fraser's cairn, at midnight, the first Monday in every month, while the season lasts. If ye neglect this my biddin, foul will befaw ye, and the fate of Walter o Rhuairm shall owertak ye; ye shall surely perish in the waste; the raven shall croak yer dirge; and yer bones shall be pickit by the eagle.'
(Words according to the story published in Scrope's Days of Deer Stalking c. 1773.)

The hunters promised to do as she has asked and then they ate and slept. In the morning the woman was gone and the storm had passed so they returned home.

There are a lot of places in Scotland where the Cailleach is associated with the red deer that live there. You will also find lots of Pictish carvings showing deer symbols.

Luan Lae Bhealtaine

A traveller came to seek the wisdom of the Cailleach, knowing that she was very old and wise and that she had lived for hundreds of years. When he met with her he asked if she could remember a particular day that happened a 100 years before, a day that was very cold, the time of year being Luan Lae

Bhealtaine (the first day of summer). The Cailleach replied that she could not remember that day specifically, but that the man should go to see the eagle that lived in the ruins of an old forge and he would maybe have the answer. The eagle was said to be 300 years older than the Cailleach and would know a lot of things that she didn't.

The man set off and eventually found the old forge and the eagle. He asked the same question that he had of the Cailleach to which the eagle replied that he had been alive for 700 years and could remember when the anvil in the forge was new and when he used to eat his food he would clean his beak by rubbing it on the peak of the anvil. The peak of the anvil was now worn away. The eagle could not remember the day that the man was enquiring about and suggested he seek out the otter that lived on a rock as he may be able to remember.

The man went off to find the rock and sure enough there was an otter sitting on top of it. The man asked the otter how cold it was on the day of Luan Lee Bhealtaine a 100 years ago. The otter replied that he had been lying on the rock for 500 years and had worn the rock down so deeply that he had made a huge dip in the centre. But he could not remember that day and recommended that the man seek out the half blind salmon of Eas Rua because he would be the only one that would know; if he didn't then no one else would.

Off the man set again, this time to Eas Rua where he found the salmon and again he asked his question. The salmon did indeed remember that day; he had leapt out of the water to catch a fly and in between leaping and landing back in the water a thick ice had formed on the river and when he fell back he landed on solid ice until a seagull flew by and saw him, taking his eye right out of the salmon's head. The bloodshed from his eye melted the ice and he was able to swim freely in the water again. That was how cold it was on that particular Luan Lae Bhealtaine day.

Note: The suggestion is that this story could relate to the first day of all time, one which the Cailleach although old could not remember. However, in seeking out her knowledge the man was given guidance from her in order to find the answer he was looking for, showing her great wisdom. The eagle, otter and salmon may also represent air, earth and water with the Cailleach being fire...just an idea.

Globe-Trotting Cailleach

The focus of stories place the Cailleach in Scotland or Ireland with her morphing into Black Annis in England, but her name can be found (possibly) in other countries. In his text Histories (431-425 BC) Herodotus mentions a tribe on the Iberian Peninsula which he called the Kallaikoi (in Greek). Strabo (7BCE-23CE) mentions the same tribe as does Pliny (77CE). Both refer to the tribe in Latin as Callaeci, while Ptolemy suggests that the meaning of this name is 'worshippers of the Cailleach'. So it is possible that the Cailleach was known originally in Spain. This tribe may have migrated to Ireland at the end of the Ice Age bringing the worship of the Cailleach with them.

When the Romans found the Callaeci tribe they called the area they lived in 'the land of the Callaeci' (not very creative, but it makes sense). That land became known as Gallaecia and then its present-day name of Galicia.

In Scandinavia there is a triple goddess called the Mo Braido, the Mamma/Omma and the Kaelling/Karring. The Karring being the old crone figure who controls the winter storms, guards fresh water wells and has a black rod that spreads ice and frost. She also has a tinderbox that produces the sparks of life. She creates the landscape by dropping boulders and stones from her apron and she lives in a cave. Over the winter she looks after the sleeping plants and is considered to be the mother of all creation looking after transformation and the cycle of life...definitely sounds like a familiar description.

There is a Norse ballad, Hermod the Young, that tells of a hero who saves a young maiden who has been captured by a giantess. He visits the mountain dwelling of the hag and is permitted to stay the night. Using his cunning he persuades the giantess the next morning to visit her neighbours. While she is gone he rescues the maiden and they flee from the house (on skis...because it is snowy). The giantess chases after them, as Hermod and the maiden come to a salt fjord with the giantess hot on their heels the giantess is suddenly turned to stone by the sun that rises just at that moment. Although in the Swedish version it is the influence of an iron cross by the fjord that turns the giantess to stone. Danish tales suggest that the maiden in the ballad is Sigri, daughter of Siward, who is carried away by a giant who is slain by Ottar. The hero loves the maiden, but she does not feel the same way and takes refuge in a hut owned by 'a certain huge woman' where she looks after the goats and the sheep. At the end of the story she marries Ottar who takes her away.

From Romania we get the story of a great witch who runs a coven of eight other witches. She sets her daughter-in-law the task of washing a brown fleece and making it white. The young lady washes the fleece in a stream, but it is hard work. Father Winter takes pity on her and takes the fleece from her, changing it to white. When she returns home with the fleece and a bunch of flowers she picks on the way the old witch is furious and gathers the other witches with her to fight against spring. Now that does sound very familiar...storms are summoned, but the sun shines through and spring triumphs over winter. The nine witches are turned into stone, which is where they sit on top of the mountain Silash in Temesvar.

The Tuatha De Danann were said to have journeyed from Scandinavia through Greece then Scotland and on to Ireland; their journey does seem to mirror some of the Cailleach history as well.

Malta has huge Neolithic megalithic structures and temples, some of which date back to 3000BCE and these were said to have been created by a giant goddess called Sansuna. She carried huge stones on her head and in her hands to create the buildings. Was this the earliest beginnings of the goddess Cailleach?

And over in Greece we have Lamia, Queen of Libya. She lived

in a cave and left to her own devices became evil and stole children. A similar story tells of Lamia the Gello who could shape-shift into a sea creature or bird and liked to eat babies. If either of these hags was killed, no plants would grow on the ground where their blood fell.

The Barclodiad-y-Gawres burial mound on the Anglesey coast, in Wales, is a chambered cairn made from five carved stones (now capped by concrete to prevent erosion), the stones are carved with spirals, cup marks and zig zag patterns. According to local folklore a giantess was carrying an apron full of boulders. When the weight became too much and the apron strings broke, the rocks fell out and created the cairn.

On the island of Jersey, although the Cailleach does not seem to appear by name, the residents have folk tales of faeries that carried stones in their aprons, which were dropped to create part of the landscape such as three menhirs at Le Clios des Tres Pierres and La Table des Marthes at La Corbiere. The same seems to apply over the water in Brittany, France, where faeries also created landscape by dropping boulders from their aprons.

The Cailleach by Any Other Name

Black Annis

Black Annis's Bower

Where down the plain the winding pathway falls
From Glenfield Vill to Lester's ancient walls,
Nature or Art with imitative power,
Far in the glenn has placed Black Annis' Bower.

An oak, the pride of all the mossy dell,
Spread its broad arms above the stony cell;
And many a bush, with hostile thorns arrayed,
Forbids the secret cavern to invade;
Whilst delving vales each way meander round,
And violet banks with redolence abound.

Here, if the uncouth song of former days
Soil not the page with Falsehood's artful lays,
Black Annis held her solitary reign,
The dread and wonder of the neighbouring plain.
The shepherd grieved to view his waning flock,
And traced his firstlings to the gloomy rock.
No vagrant children culled (the) flow'rets then,
For infant blood oft stained the gory den.

Not Sparta's mount, for infant tears renown'd,
Echo'd more frequently the piteous sound.
Oft the gaunt Maid the frantic Mother curs'd,
Whom Britain's wolf with savage nipple nurs'd;
Whom Lester's sons beheld, aghast the scene,
Nor dared to meet the Monster of the Green.

'Tis said the soul of mortal man recoil'd,
To view Black Annis' eye, so fierce and wild;
Vast talons, foul with human flesh, there grew
In place of hands, and features livid blue
Glar'd in her visage; while the obscene waist
Warm skins of human victims close embraced.

But Time, than Man more certain, tho' more slow,
At length 'gainst Annis drew his sable bow;
The great decree the pious shepherds bless'd,
And general joy the general fear confess'd.
Not without terror they the cave survey,
Where hung the monstrous trophies of her sway:
'Tis said, that in the rock large rooms were found,
Scoop'd with her claws beneath the flinty ground;
In these the swains her hated body threw,
But left the entrance still to future view,
That children's children might the tale rehearse,
And bards record it in their tuneful verse.

But in these listless days, the idle bard
Gives to the wind all themes of cold regard;
Forgive, then, if in rough, unpolished song,
An unskilled swain the dying tale prolong.

And you, ye Fair, whom Nature's scenes delight,
If Annis' Bower your vagrant steps invite,
Ere the bright sun Aurora's car succeed,
Or dewy evening quench the thirsty mead,
Forbear with chilling censures to refuse
Some gen'rous tribute to the rustic muse.
A violet or common daisy throw,
Such gifts as Maro's lovely nymphs bestow;
Then shall your Bard survive the critic's frown,

And in your smiles enjoy his best renown.
John Heyrick – 1742-97

In England the area of Leicester carries the tale of an old hag woman dressed in black who lived in a cave. The Leicester Chronicle newspaper carried this description in 1874:

Little children who went to run on the Dane Hills, were assured that she lay in wait there, to snatch them away to her 'bower' where she scratched them to death with her claws, sucked their blood, and hung up their skins out to dry.

The newspaper ran an investigation to see if the stories were based on fact or fiction.

The poem above was written by John Heyrick, a lieutenant in the 15th Regiment of Light Dragoons, and was apparently credited as an upstanding man and a courageous soldier. Heyrick fully believed that his poem was based on historical accuracy and was a true story.

According to Heyrick, the bower (cave) belonging to Black Annis lay between Leicester and Glenfield in an area called the Dane Hills. Investigations have confirmed that the cave did indeed exist there along with the oak tree that stood over the entrance. Sadly it has now all be built over with a large housing estate.

His description of Black Annis says she was large with blue skin and one eye...sound familiar? I also wonder (and it has been suggested by others) whether there is a connection between the name Annis and the goddess Anu or Danu/Dana – another ancient mother goddess. Perhaps Black Annis is a crone aspect? Although in the following tale a dead cat was used in a celebration. The cat was doused in aniseed (anise), which was believed to avert the evil eye and protect against bad spirits. Perhaps there is a link between the name Annis and aniseed?

Cats were believed to transform into witches...

Many years before Heyrick's poem emerged, the town of Leicester held a celebration on Easter Monday in which the town leaders would visit Black Annis' bower to witness the trailing of a cat before a pack of hounds (ewww). This celebration was to welcome in the spring, and was recorded by historian Throsby:

The morning was spent in various amusements and athletic exercises, till a dead cat, about noon, was prepared by aniseed water, for commencing the mock hunting of the hare. In about half an hour after the cat had been trailed from the tail of a horse over the grounds, in zigzag directions, the hounds were directed to the spot where the cat had been trailed from. Here the hounds gave tongue, in glorious concert. The people from the various eminences, who had placed themselves to behold the sight, with shouts of rapture, gave applause; the horsemen, dashing after the hounds through foul passages and over fences, were emulous for taking the lead of their fellows. It was a scene, upon the whole, of joy; the governing and the governed, in the habits of freedom, enjoying together an innocent and recreating amusement, serving to unite them in bonds of mutual friendship, rather than to embitter their days with discord and disunion. As the cat had been trailed to the mayor's door, through some of the principle streets, consequently the dogs and horsemen followed. After the hunt was over, the mayor gave a handsome treat to his friends. In this manner the day ended.

The stories of Black Annis seem to be centred in and around the area of Leicester, but all suggest that she is a hag, a bringer of death and the winter. In all the tales she is described as being extremely tall with blue skin and usually with talons and/or long teeth and one eye, and she generally favours the bad habit of eating people, especially children. She was often blamed for the death or disappearance of livestock. She would wait in her cave ready to pounce on any children that wandered too far from the village. Once she devoured the children she would hang their skins out to dry. Perhaps this was a bit of an embellishment on the story to stop children from misbehaving?

I do think maybe she was the goddess that looked after the souls of those children that passed away too young. And perhaps also as the culler for herds of animals, taking the lives of those that were weak allowing the strongest to survive?

The townsfolk of Leicester would lock and bar their doors and windows when they heard the howling of Black Annis. They would tie bunches of herbs above the windows to stop her reaching inside and stealing their babies.

I find, interestingly, that a lot of the descriptions of Black Annis also echo those of the Hindu goddess Kali. Was Black Annis the English version of the Cailleach? I like to think so, but the decision is yours to make.

Gyre Carling

In lowland parts of Scotland the Cailleach is referred to as the Gyre Carling. 'Gyre' is a Scandinavian word meaning giantess and 'carling' or 'carlin' is the Scottish equivalent to the Gaelic word 'Cailleach'. It is usually understood that both the Gyre Carling and the Cailleach are one and the same being. However, the Gyre Carling is also said to have been able to take the form of a beautiful Witch Queen of the Unseelie court of faeries. She was supposed to have been worshipped by the Scottish witches and 16th century witchcraft trial documents make reference to her, including the statement that she could be young or old at will. She is said to ride out every Halloween at the head of her spirit army or the Wild Hunt. Tales tell that when the Gyre Carling is attacked she turns into a pig and runs away. She is also said to carry an iron club (presumably not when she is in pig form). An old poem also states that the Gyre Carling lived on men's flesh. There does seem to be reference in a lot of articles that the Gyre Carling is also referred to as the Nicnevin, but I personally think she is a separate deity.

Nicneven

In a few of the stories I found mention of the goddess Nicneven as being associated with or corresponding to the Cailleach. The Nicneven being a Scottish Samhain goddess, her name translates from Gaelic as 'daughter of the little saint' or some say 'daughter of Neamhain/Morrigan'. 'Nic' often means 'daughter of' and maybe the 'neven' part of her name refers to Ben Nevis? I don't have a definitive answer, I am just sharing some of the possibilities.

Nicneven is described as a hag and one that was in the habit of night riding. Stories tell that she rides out from the mountain Ben Nevis with her eight sister hags at the end of summer to hammer the frost into the ground...another tale that is awfully similar to that told of the Cailleach.

Nicneven is also known as the Queen of Elphame, the world of Faerie.

Both Nicneven and the Cailleach are elemental goddesses whose power grows stronger as the days grow shorter, they both fly out from Ben Nevis and they both carry a wand of power that shapes the land and the weather.

Are they one and the same? I am not convinced, but you can make your own decision, perhaps this may be a reflection of the Cailleach and her younger alter ego.

A folklorist called Walter Traill Dennison recorded a 'Witches Charm' in the 1880s from the Orkneys in Scotland. It seems to be a dedication ritual to the gods and the 'dark witch'.

The instructions given are: During the full moon, go to a solitary beach by the sea. Turn yourself around three times witherlins/against the sun and lay down on the beach at the ebb the area between high and low tide. Place a stone at each of your outstretched hands and feet, one at the head, one at the chest, and one over the heart totalling seven stones. Speak aloud:

O' Mester King o' a' that's ill,
Come fill me wi' the Warlock's Skill,
An' I shall serve wi' all me will.
Trow take me gin I sinno!
Trow take me gin I winno!
Trow take me win I cinno!
Come take me noo, an take me a',
Take lights an' liver, pluck and ga,
Take me, take me, noo I say,
Fae de how o' da heed, tae da tip o' da tae.
Take a' dats oot an' in o' me.
Take hare an hide an a' tae thee.
Take hert, an harns, flesh, bleud and banes,
Take a' atween the seeven stanes,I' de name of da muckle black
Wallowa!

The translation:

O Master King of all that's ill,
Come fill me with the Witches' Skill,
And I shall serve with all my will.
Devil take me if I sin!
Devil take me if I fly!
Devil take me when I cannot!
Come take me now, and take me all,
Take lungs and liver, organs and feet,
Take me, take me, now I say!
From the brow of the head, to the tip of the toe.
Take all that's out and in of me.
Take hair and hide and all to thee.
Take heart and brains, flesh, blood and bones,
Take all between the seven stones!
In the name of the great dark witch!

Lie quietly and meditate for a few moments, then open your

eyes, turn on your left side, rise and throw each stone individually into the sea crying a malediction with each one.

Who the 'Master King' was, no one is sure. It could refer to Manannan, but the assumption is that the 'dark witch' makes reference to Nicneven. It has also been suggested that some of the lines have been added or changed from the original and some words may have been misheard or mis-recorded, particularly the word 'wallowa'. This is found in Scottish dialect, but refers to the Devil. It would seem more likely that the word was not properly recognised and may have been the old Norse word 'volva', which means prophetess or witch.

Glaistig

This supernatural being from Scotland has a lot of Cailleach characteristics. The Glaistig is a solitary being with a body that is half woman (the upper) and half goat (the lower) although she was able to appear in either form as a whole. She had long blonde hair and pale grey skin, often seen in a long green flowing robe (presumably to cover her hairy legs…).

She could be found by lochs and rivers with her name actually meaning 'water imp'. She was apparently both benevolent and malevolent towards people, sometimes even taking on the role of Banshee to wail at the impending death. She was also known to be a trickster who would tease travellers and lead them astray. But she could also be a friend to children, spending time with them in play. Some stories credit her with owning a magic wand similar to that of the Cailleach.

The Glaistig was connected closely with cattle and wild deer. Offerings of milk were poured onto the earth and stones for her. One story tells of a village on the Isle of Mull where the Glaistig protected the cattle. The only payment she asked for in return was an offering of milk poured into a holey stone. One mischievous young boy decided to play a joke and poured boiling hot milk into the stone. The Glaistig burnt her tongue on the hot milk and was so angry that she left the herd and was never seen again.

Another story from the Isle of Mull tells of a family whose herd of cattle was protected by the Glaistig. One day raiders came to steal the animals, but the Glaistig in her fury inadvertently struck the cows and turned them into stone, this broke her heart and she died. The stone cattle can still be seen in the Heroes Hollow (Glaic nan Gaisgeach).

Also like the Cailleach she would often wade through deep water or cross oceans and rivers by stepping from island to island.

Sheela Na Gig

A figure of a woman holding open her vulva with both hands can often be seen carved into stone on churches and castles and in my research I have seen the occasional suggestion that this may be symbolic of the Cailleach once she has been turned into stone. While the Sheela Na Gig is an ancient goddess, I personally don't feel there is a connection, but it may resonate with you.

Frau Holda/Holle

The Germanic goddess Frau Holda (sometimes called Holle) shares a lot of similarities with the Cailleach in her characteristics and stories. She is seen as a maiden, but also a mother and a hag, she brings storms, leads the Wild Hunt and both protects and steals the souls of children. She appreciates those who work hard, but punishes the lazy. And, of course, the Frau is a goddess of winter bringing the first snow as she is said to pluck her geese and shake the goose feathers out of the window and onto the ground. The rain is her doing the washing, the lightning is her scotching the flax and the fog is the smoke from her chimney. Frau Holda is also believed by some to be the patron goddess of witches and magic and a goddess of the Underworld and the Faery folk.

The Loathly Lady

If you wish to make the connection…the idea of the Cailleach and some of her stories have followed through into more modern literature. Variations on a theme appear such as the Nine Hostages story given in this book for instance: Niall and his brothers searching for a well that is guarded by a hag who asks for a kiss, the reward for it being sovereignty of Ireland and the hag turning into a beautiful woman.

Then there is the tale of The Wedding of Sir Gawain and Dame Ragnelle. In this story it is Gawain who agrees to marry the hideous Ragnelle who provides him with the answer to a riddle, 'What do women most desire,' to prevent the death of King Arthur. Seriously that has to be the most difficult riddle ever. Even as a woman I don't always know what I want! And then the Wife of Bath's Tale where the Loathly Lady appears to a knight in the court of King Arthur. The knight must face execution if he doesn't answer that same riddle and the Loathly Lady giving him the option of marrying her for the answer. All are variations on a theme and all can possibly be traced back to stories of the Cailleach.

Priestess Cult

There are suggestions that there was an ancient Cailleach priestess cult as she was, it seems, a major part of several tribal groups who brought her worship with them. Also, all of the land-shaping stories would seem to suggest a supernatural being that may have been formed into something that could have had its own priesthood following. Throw in the association with water, her shape-shifting ability and sacred wells along with her ancient roots and cronehood – perhaps the priestesses themselves were of the crone age.

Mackay wrote an essay in 1932 titled The Deer-Cult and the Deer Goddess Cult of the Ancient Caledonians, in which he put forward the idea that there was an ancient priestess cult in Scotland at one time who were associated with the protection and care of the deer herds there. He gives the name of the cult as the Cailleach Mhor Nam Fiadh or 'Cailleachan'. He suggests that a group of seven giant women from Jura protected the deer herds. He also puts forward the idea that there was an island of 'big women', which was situated in the middle of Loch nam Ban Mora, which could only be accessed by stepping stones that were so far apart only giants could use them.

Working Magic with The Cailleach

Because of the lack of records telling us how the ancient peoples worshipped the Cailleach there aren't really any 'traditional' symbols or correspondences, but the following should give you some idea, these are my personal opinions:

Aspects/Attributes: Balance, rebirth, cycles, endurance, overcoming hardship, honesty, winter, harvest, autumn, night, wind, seas, nature, storms

Element: Earth

Colours: Grey, blue, black, silver, white, brown

Herbs and Plants: Woodruff, witch hazel, hazel, hazel nuts, rue, patchouli, honeysuckle, holly, elm, elder, pansy, poppy, rose, tansy, yew, clove, pine, St John's wort, snapdragon, magnolia

Stones: Rough stones, grey agate, turquoise, blue howlite, pebbles, shells, sea glass

Animals: Cats, deer, wolves, owls, cattle, swine, wild boar, goats, ravens, crows

Symbols: Hammers, rocks, snow, hills, wands, blue, deer, mountains, earth, skulls, spirals, the waning moon, falling leaves

Places: Mountains, rivers, lakes, streams, rocky places, megalithic temples, standing stones, wells, the ocean, marshes

Suggested Offerings: Pebbles, hag stones, shells, feathers, boiled sweets (she is an old lady, they always like boiled sweets)

Using a hag stone (holey stone), a pebble or a shell – just sit for a few moments in silence and connect with the earth energies of the stone to bring you balance and connection to the strength of the Cailleach.

Feed the birds in your garden or local park, this is a way of connecting with the goddess and also offering thanks.

Any craft item made with stones, shells or pebbles would be perfect to honour the Cailleach. Even something simple like painting a spiral shape on a large flat pebble.

Make a pebble and shell altar in your garden to honour her. This is very simple to do – just make a pretty pile of pebbles and shells.

Use small shells and glue them to an old picture frame.

Create a pebble or shell spiral in your garden.

Write inspirational words or affirmations onto pebbles and keep them in a dish in your home.

If you have hag stones (holey stones) thread them onto pretty ribbon and hang them over a doorway for positive energy and good luck.

Using wire, wrap shells and pebbles and make a wind chime decoration for the garden.

Lessons from the Cailleach

The Cailleach can teach us many things, such as:

The sense of life, death and rebirth – the cycle of life
Protection, as she looks after the earth in its deepest slumber
*Life must go on even if threads are cut you can mend them and move
    forward*
Never fear
*Let go of the old and that which holds you back to be able to move
    forward*
Release
Work with empathy, love and compassion
Whatever you are doing, give it your all
Wisdom
Guidance
Strength
Look beneath the surface
Trust
Shape-shifting – you can be whatever you want to be
Inner beauty
Transformation.
Knowledge from our ancestors
The importance of nature and our planet
Magic
Balance
Overcoming obstacles
Receiving forgiveness
Releasing of guilt

She is a dark goddess, but you need to see and understand the
dark to be able to appreciate and balance with the light. The dark
is a place of shadow and mystery and can be seen as something

that we fear. The Cailleach can help us to see into that darkness and not be afraid. However, she also has her own light compassionate side as well.

As she is associated with 'veils', the Cailleach helps to remind us that we all hide behind veils or put on masks at some time, perhaps too much of the time. We hide the truth locked away inside. We not only hide things from others, but also from ourselves. Perhaps the veil is there because we aren't ready to share, perhaps the veil has been there too long...the tricky part is recognising when to reveal our true selves to others if at all, but I think we should always be true to your own self, the Cailleach can help with that.

The Cailleach is a goddess of fresh and salt water in the form of oceans, rivers, lakes, streams and wells. Water is cleansing and purifying and is most definitely linked to our emotions. Water also has an element of danger, especially oceans and the power that they have. Never underestimate the strength of water. The Cailleach can help you overcome fear and help you deal with emotions, bringing cleansing and purification with her.

The shore at the beach or around a lake is a place of 'in between'; it is a boundary between the water and the earth and is therefore a very magical place, a spot of transformation and enlightenment.

She is also a goddess of the land, the earth, the mountains and the rocks; this gives her a balance between water and earth. She provides grounding and stability and the wisdom of the ancestors.

From my own personal experience with the Cailleach you cannot be lazy or ignore her advice, she will enforce it. She can act in what might seem harsh ways, but they are all lessons. You may not want them, but you certainly need them.

Cailleach Ritual

Holding onto negative feelings can not only make you feel miserable, it can also manifest in physical ways too. Don't hold onto it. Forgive yourself, let go of guilt and negative emotions and move on. If you cannot forgive yourself or others then you cannot heal yourself.

The Cailleach is wise and can see through any veils you pull across. She is the power of the ocean, which can cleanse, purify and release. As a crone she is often represented by a spiral, it is this symbol that can help you let go.

If you can do this on a beach it would be perfect, but obviously that might not be possible. With a bit of visualisation and creativity this can be done in your garden or home.

You will need to create a spiral, be creative, whether you draw it on paper or create it by drawing a spiral shape in sand or rice; you could even create a spiral shape with pebbles, shells or crystals. Use a bowl of sea or salt water as your central point for the spiral.

Cast your circle by walking deosil (clockwise) around your space three times. While you do this, visualise a protective bubble surrounding you.

Face each direction in turn to call in the elements; you could even place a lighted candle at each quarter.

I call to the east, the element of air
Chill winds and icy blasts
The intellect carried by the birds of the sea
Hail and welcome

I call to the south, the element of fire
Island volcanoes and shoreline fires
Bring your passion and energy

Hail and welcome

I call to the west, the element of water
The oceans, the rivers
The intuition of the wells and springs
Hail and welcome

I call to the north, the element of earth
The rocks, the mountains
The stability of the earth
Hail and welcome

Then face the centre:

Cailleach, mother of stone and bone, we call to you
Lady of keening, bringer of the seasons
Keeper of mysteries and the cauldron of hidden sight
Come dark mother and aid us in parting the veil
We invite you to join our circle and ask for your blessings
Hail and welcome

You will need to have six, nine or 12 small pebbles or shells to hold in your hand. Look at the spiral and say out loud:

I journey on this spiral to leave behind any guilt and shame that I am holding onto and to bring back my self-worth and positive energy.

Then if you are able to walk the spiral, do so. If not, then you can trace the spiral you have created with your finger.

Start at the outer edge and work inwards as you walk or trace drop a pebble or shell at intervals; allow these pebbles to release your guild and negative emotions as they fall.

When you have dropped all your pebbles and have reached

the centre, dip your fingers in the salt water and anoint your forehead for wisdom, your throat for freedom of speech and your heart for release of all guilt and to bring you self love and self worth.

Take a few moments to connect with the Cailleach and listen to any wise words she has for you, then slowly return back out of the spiral.

Thank the Cailleach for joining you and bid her: *'Hail and farewell.'*

Turn to each direction and thank them for lending their energies to the rite and bid them hail and farewell.

Walk widdershins (anti clockwise) around the circle stating out loud: *'This circle is open but never broken. Blessed be.'*

Pour the water from the bowl onto the sand or soil and place the pebbles/shells on the soil or onto the sand.

If you feel guilt rising again at any time, remind yourself of this rite or visualise the spiral in your mind.

Meditation to Meet the Cailleach

Make yourself comfortable in a place where you won't be disturbed. Close your eyes and begin to focus on your breathing. Take deep breaths in…and out.

The world around you dissipates and you find yourself on a hillside, the air is biting cold and the ground beneath your feet is covered in a fresh white blanket of snow. However, you don't feel the cold as you are wrapped in a warm woollen cloak, which you pull closer around you.

You listen, but there are no sounds, just the silence of a land in slumber beneath the snow.

Take a look around you and notice the landscape, the mountains in the distance and the scattering of lone trees all standing bare against the backdrop of snow. The sky is blue and the weak winter sun is trying its best to warm the land.

As you look around you notice what looks like the entrance to a cave and a slight waft of smoke drifting out from within so you start to make your way towards it.

Your feet crunch in the crisp white snow and your breath turns to mist as you breathe. As you walk you notice a few large black crows are circling above high in the blue sky.

As you draw near to the cave entrance you can smell the smoke from a wood fire. It is dark inside the cave, but you enter hesitantly.

A voice calls out to you from the inner cavern inviting you to come in.

You follow the voice and the smoke to see an old woman hunched over a cauldron hanging above a wood fire. She beckons you to sit down.

You sit in silence for a short while, watching the smoke from the fire and the old woman stirring the contents of the cauldron. Then she stops and comes to sit beside you. She takes your hand in hers and looks at you. Her eyes are full of knowledge and wisdom and so very ancient she holds the mysteries of all time.

Ask her what you need to know...listen to her answer very carefully...

When you are finished she reaches into her pocket and hands you a gift, a reminder of what you have talked about. You take it and thank her.

When you are ready you say farewell and rise, leaving the warmth and darkness of the cave without looking back.

You walk back across the snow-covered hillside to the point where you arrived.

Slowly and gently come back to the here and now, wriggle your fingers and toes and open your eyes.

Have a drink and something to eat and write down the message that the Cailleach gave to you.

The Wicked Witch

So why was the Cailleach portrayed as evil in so many of the stories? I don't have a definitive answer, but I will share my thoughts with you. When Christianity came to Britain, some of the stories may have been changed to make out that the pagan deities were evil...leave the dark side and come into the light kinda thing.

But there is also the belief that people had in the Craft. Warriors and even kings would be worried if they were crossed or cursed by an old woman believed to be a witch. It was powerful stuff and could spook an entire army to know that they had been cursed, so the 'old hag' had great power which those in charge didn't like. Portraying the old woman as the 'bad guy' in stories was one way of counteracting this fear.

Working folk would also have been ruled by kings and landlords who were rich and powerful, the poor people feeling resentful would also have sought protection and magic spells from the local 'wise woman' thus giving the peasants a power of sorts. Any soldier or warrior meeting an old woman on his travels would think twice about offending her in case she worked the Craft on him. Again the stories that turned the wise woman into an evil figure would help those rich and powerful to beat down the ideas from the peasants that they had any power at all.

In Summary

My journey with the Cailleach has been enlightening, eventful, rewarding and sometimes hard but it continues and each day I learn something new. I hope this book has given you some insight and hopefully a connection with her. As with all deities the journey I have with her will be different to yours, but I can tell you it will be exciting and very, very worthwhile.

She is the crone, but also the mother and the maiden – she is all things, she is in all things, she is the goddess.

References

If you are interested in the written sources of some of these folk stories here are some essays, documents and manuscripts to look up:

A Highland Goddess – Mackenzie (1912)

A Manx Scrapbook – Gill (1929)

Callanish: The Stones and Moon and the Sacred Landscape – Curtis & Curtis (1994)

Examples of Printed Folklore Concerning Fife – Simpkins (1914)

Legends and Traditions of the Cailleach Bheara – Hull (1927)

Myth, Tradition and Story from Western Argyll – Grant (1925)

Myths of Babylonia & Assyria – Mackenzie (1915)

Pagan Celtic Britain – Ross (1967)

Popular Tales of the West Highlands & Islands of Scotland – Campbell (1860)

Scenes and Legends of the North of Scotland – Miller (1835)

Superstitions of the Highlands & Islands of Scotland – Campbell (1900)

The Book of the Cailleach – O'Crualaoich (2003)

The Deer Cult and the Deer Goddess Cult of the Ancient Caledonians – Mackay (1932)

The Early Races of Scotland and Their Monuments – Leslie (1868)

The Fairy Tradition in Britain – Lewis Spence

Witchcraft & Second Sight in the Highlands & Islands of Scotland – Campbell (1902)

Wonder Tales from Scottish Myth and Legend – Mackenzie (1917)

Yellow Book of Lecan (14thC)

Moon Books invites you to begin or deepen your encounter with Paganism, in all its rich, creative, flourishing forms.

If you have enjoyed this book, why not tell other readers by posting a review on your preferred booksite. Recent bestsellers from Moon Books are:

Journey to the Dark Goddess
How to Return to Your Soul
Jane Meredith
Discover the powerful secrets of the Dark Goddess and transform your depression, grief and pain into healing and integration.
Paperback: 978-1-84694-677-6
ebook: 978-1-78099-223-5

Shamanic Reiki
Expanded Ways of Working with Universal Life Force Energy
Llyn Roberts, Robert Levy
Shamanism and Reiki are each powerful ways of healing; together, their power multiplies. Shamanic Reiki introduces techniques to help healers and Reiki practitioners tap ancient healing wisdom.
Paperback: 978-1-84694-037-8
ebook: 978-1-84694-650-9

Pagan Portals – The Awen Alone
Walking the Path of the Solitary Druid
Joanna van der Hoeven
An introductory guide for the solitary Druid, The Awen Alone will accompany you as you explore and seek out your own place within the natural world.
Paperback: 978-1-78279-547-6
ebook: 978-1-78279-546-9

A Kitchen Witch's World of Magical Herbs & Plants
Rachel Patterson
A journey into the magical world of herbs and plants, filled with magical uses, folklore, history and practical magic. By popular writer, blogger and kitchen witch, Tansy Firedragon.
Paperback: 978-1-78279-621-3
ebook: 978-1-78279-620-6

Medicine for the Soul
The Complete Book of Shamanic Healing
Ross Heaven
All you will ever need to know about shamanic healing and how to become your own shaman...
Paperback: 978-1-78099-419-2
ebook: 978-1-78099-420-8

Shaman Pathways – The Druid Shaman
Exploring the Celtic Otherworld
Danu Forest
A practical guide to Celtic shamanism with exercises and techniques as well as traditional lore for exploring the Celtic Otherworld.
Paperback: 978-1-78099-615-8
ebook: 978-1-78099-616-5

Traditional Witchcraft for the Woods and Forests
A Witch's Guide to the Woodland with Guided Meditations and Pathworking
Melusine Draco
A Witch's guide to walking alone in the woods, with guided meditations and pathworking.
Paperback: 978-1-84694-803-9
ebook: 978-1-84694-804-6

Wild Earth, Wild Soul
A Manual for an Ecstatic Culture
Bill Pfeiffer
Imagine a nature-based culture so alive and so connected,
spreading like wildfire. This book is the first flame...
Paperback: 978-1-78099-187-0
ebook: 978-1-78099-188-7

Naming the Goddess
Trevor Greenfield
Naming the Goddess is written by more than 80 adherents and
scholars of the Goddess and Goddess Spirituality.
Paperback: 978-1-78279-476-9
ebook: 978-1-78279-475-2

Shapeshifting into Higher Consciousness
Heal and transform yourself and our world with ancient and
modern Shamanic methods.
Llyn Roberts
Ancient and modern methods that you can use every day
to transform yourself and make a positive difference in the
world.
Paperback: 978-1-84694-843-5
ebook: 978-1-84694-844-2

**Find more titles and sign up to our readers' newsletter at
http://www.johnhuntpublishing.com/paganism.
Follow us on Facebook at
https://www.facebook.com/MoonBooks and Twitter at
https://twitter.com/MoonBooksJHP. Most titles are
published in paperback and as an ebook. Paperbacks are
available in physical bookshops. Both print and ebook
editions are available online. Readers of ebooks can
click on the live links in the titles to order.**